Symbols
of
Inner Truth

Uncovering the Spiritual Meaning of Experience

Carole Marie Kelly, O.S.F.

Paulist Press ◆ New York ◆ Mahwah, N.J.

Library of Congress Cataloging-in-Publication Data

Kelly, Carole Marie.
     Symbols of inner truth.

     1. Spiritual life.   I. Title.
BV4501.2.K4265   1988   248   88-25372
ISBN 0-8091-0424-5 (cloth)

Published by Paulist Press
997 Macarthur Boulevard
Mahwah, New Jersey 07430

Printed and bound in the
United States of America

Contents

Acknowledgements

Through the years many people have led me to recognize the symbols of my inner truth, to uncover their meaning, and to follow their wisdom. All of these persons have contributed to this book, and while it is impossible to mention all of them, I thank them.

There are two individuals, however, who have had a direct influence on these pages, and I want to acknowledge them in a special way. One is Al Ross, Ph.D., who opened the doors to the inner world of my dreams and guided me in my first exploration of that realm, teaching me to listen to my God in a new way. It was Al who first suggested that I share my experiences in writing.

Another person who has contributed significantly to this book is Bruno Barnhart, Cam.O.S.B., who has guided me in my journey into solitude. The wisdom and spiritual insight that he has shared along the way have enriched my life and given me the confidence to continue the journey. He has also reviewed each chapter of the book and made invaluable suggestions along the way.

Introduction

The pond lay shimmering in the gentle morning sunlight, encircled by the stillness of the wooded hills. Bird songs echoed from tree to tree greeting the sun as it rose in the soft blue sky. It was a moment of quiet that draws forth reflections from deep within the heart.

I pensively tossed a pebble into the center of the pond, and then another and another, watching the rippled rings slide gently across the mirrored surface and disappear.

It reminded me of what happens when I read a book. So often one sentence can trigger a movement of ideas and memories within me. I stop reading and allow that to happen, watching the rippling thoughts extend out over the surface of my mind. Then as the pebble sinks into the pond of my unconscious it seems to touch my inner Self, the place where God dwells. At that center point of my being I am affected in a way that I cannot explain or describe. I hear an inner voice that speaks in the form of images or feelings that surface to my consciousness. If I am attentive, these gradually become realizations, and questions that I can ponder. Then the cycle is complete. They are transformed into pebbles that I once again toss into the pond.

Tossing pebbles into a pond is a symbol of an inner process, an image that expresses an intuition that cannot be adequately formulated in words, although that is what I have just attempted to do. Symbol comes from the Greek word "sumballein" meaning "to throw together." It brings together the visible and the invisible, the conscious and the unconscious, an intuition and an idea, creating a greater unity and wholeness within a person.

Symbols of our inner truth may be images, happenings, objects or sounds; they may be noticed in dreams, in art forms or in the most ordinary experience. Whatever their form, they express a profound meaning that is beyond the grasp of words. By becoming aware of them we allow them to reveal a wisdom which may be transformed into a conscious insight, or which may simply affect us without words.

Symbols, like pebbles, come in many sizes, shapes and colors. Here they will take the form of scriptural images, personal experiences and dreams held together by themes familiar to all who undertake the spiritual journey. In each chapter the symbols focus on a different topic such as discernment, solitude, fear, options, self-knowledge, relationships, acceptance, the present moment, prayer, and desire.

As you read, I hope that circles of movement will be created in your own thoughts, and that the pebbles will descend to touch your deepest center. Then the symbols of your own inner truth will come to mind. Stay with the symbol and learn to have confidence in its message.

The story is told that one night a brother who was traveling with Francis of Assisi decided to stay awake to observe how he prayed. All night long he heard Francis repeat only two questions, "Who are you, God?" and "Who am I?" Those are the only two questions worth asking, and it will take not only a lifetime, but an eternity to grasp the answer. It is the response to one that enables us to hear the response to the other. To know our true Self is to know God, and to know our God is to know our Self. It is essential that we recognize the voice of our true Self and of our God. "I bless Yahweh, who is my Counselor, and in the night my inmost self instructs me" (Ps 16:7). Our inmost Self often speaks the language of symbol, and too often we, therefore, overlook its wisdom.

Psychology and spirituality, life experience and prayer attune us to our own truth and lead us to a greater understanding of who we are that we may be more truly ourselves, conforming to the image and likeness of God that lies deep within us.

The insights that I share with you in these pages are thoughts and questions spoken by my own inner voice. They have been given to me to be shared, so I offer them to you—a handful of pebbles. Hold them quietly and then toss them prayerfully into your own inner pond.

1

HOIST A SIGNAL

As we came to the top of the mountain and turned off the paved road toward the gate that led into the private property, I noticed a line of mailboxes stretched across a weathered beam. The words "The Hoist" were carved into the wood which was balanced on an antique, iron hoist. We continued on a narrow, dirt road that curved around the mountainside for a half mile until we came to a small cabin that had been offered to me to rent as a hermitage.

That night when I arrived home, tired, with pros and cons about the safety and suitability of the cabin jostling in my mind, I went to my prayer space and attempted to quiet my thoughts. Impatient to know what I should do, I was led to turn to the words of scripture for guidance. I opened the Bible first to Isaiah 13:1, "On a bare hill hoist a signal." I was astounded! On the opposite page the words "They do no hurt, no harm on all my holy mountain" seemed to leap out at me. What more assurance that I should move there did I need? But I had decided to open both the Old and the New Testaments, so I hesitantly opened the Bible once more, almost fearing that my bubble would pop if I did not receive as clear a message there. The account of the transfiguration was before me. I immediately associated the presence of Elijah with the fact that the cabin was near the small town of Carmel. Another clear sign.

I seldom use scripture like this, asking that God lead me in such a concrete way to answers to my dilemmas, and I do not encourage others to do so. The fact that I was moved to pray for guidance that night by opening the Bible is as significant as the words I read. First I had to be open to hearing the silent word the Spirit was speaking within me; only

7

then could I be led to the symbolic message I was meant to read in the words of scripture.

The language God uses to speak to us is like that, a merging of words, symbols and silence. So also is the language of our true Self. In my own experience I no longer struggle with naming the message that comes to me as coming from my true Self or from God. My true Self is the image of God in which I was created, and the God within me sometimes speaks through that authentic Self. What matters is that I learn to hear and understand the message, and discern its truth. The message of the Self is entwined with God's will, the words of the Holy Spirit—however one wants to refer to that encounter with the Divine.

The discipline of learning the language of that inner voice, so that it may be distinguished from the other voices such as selfishness, fear and pride, is a lifelong process. The silent communications can be deceptive. They may seem to be merely meditative reflections or thoughts and ideas that spring from the rational level. Still there is sometimes a sense that the realizations which surface come from a source deeper than one's own thinking. The communication can even be channeled through external events and symbols.

The question then arises, "How do I know if I am really listening to God, to my deepest Self, or if the thoughts that come are only a musing of my conscious mind, a daydream, or a logical consideration of facts? How do I know if I am making it all up? Am I really understanding my inner language which sometimes speaks in symbols or even in silence, which even uses external signs to speak the message?" The litmus test of this communication is often the impact it has on the person. Musings and daydreams are usually soon forgotten, leaving behind little trace of their presence. On the other hand, we frequently know if we have released an inner truth by the effect of the message received. This may manifest itself in many different ways, such as:

- by the sense of wonder and awe created within us,
- by a sudden realization or insight that seems to have no connection with our previous thoughts or experience,
- by a fear or reluctance to accept what we hear,
- by the sense of peace and at-oneness we experience,
- by the numinous power that remains within us.

One clue to the validity of the message is the strength of the impact or conscious reaction to the communication. Another clue is that it often indicates a direction we must take in our lives, or even leads to an inner transformation. Yet sometimes in order to be sure we must wait for later validation of the communication through synchronistic happenings or other experiences.

For example, after I had interpreted the appearance of Elijah in my reading of the account of the transfiguration as a sign that I was meant to move to Carmel, references to Elijah continued to haunt me for a month. I still refer to that series of happenings as "my Elijah experience." I would be browsing in a bookstore, take a book off the shelf and open it to a chapter about Elijah; readings at Mass and in the Office mentioned the prophet several times. Once I smiled as I picked up the autobiography of St. Thérèse, thinking that here at least I would not find a reference to Elijah. Yes, even Thérèse spoke to me of him. Then, as if to add a note of comic relief, the culmination of this series of synchronistic events came one day while I was having dinner at a retreat house. I dropped an olive which rolled across the table to the gentleman sitting opposite me. He smiled, picked it up and put it at the empty place next to him saying simply, "This is for Elijah." After such repeated messages, of course I moved to Carmel!

Validation of our understanding of God's will for us seldom takes such persistent, concrete form, but God knows our weakness and hesitancy, and treats us accordingly, sending many reassurances. An external sign such as a word of encouragement from a friend, an article in the newspaper, or an unexpected telephone call can be a confirmation of the message of the inner voice.

We must be cautious in our discernment of inner truth and interpretations of external signs—not so much because of the danger that the truth is not spoken within us, but because of our tendency to inject our own hopes or fears into the interpretation.

On the other hand, we can all remember times of tension when we wanted to do something that would move our lives in a different direction, but we hesitated to take the risk and chose rather to listen to the differing expectations of family, friends, or common sense. It seemed safer, more prudent. We are conditioned by our earliest training in family and school to conform to others' wishes and deny our own impulses. To an extent this is an important part of the socialization process. The immature person needs structure and guidelines while developing a secure ego, a sense of self. The unfortunate aspect of this developmental process is that some never learn to let go of the security of living up to others' expectations in order to become the individual persons they were created to be. Their self-worth is based on pleasing others and achieving success according to others' standards rather than upon being themselves. "Being yourself" is too often negatively labeled as "doing your own thing," or "being self-centered."

This, of course, is a danger. But how can we know the difference between responding to our true Self by doing what God asks of us, and being self-centered? There is no facile answer to that question. After we have reflected and done all that we can to understand the meaning of the word we hear, we should sometimes seek guidance and reassurance from another person experienced in discernment. This is not to imply that another can independently tell us what is being spoken within us. The function of the guide or spiritual director is simply to assist us in the process of understanding the messages that come from our inner Self, and to offer us confirmation and support. The individual must find his or her own way by learning to listen to the words and decode the language spoken.

At the same time, it is important to develop confidence in the inner guide. In the Christian tradition we speak of the gift of wisdom, the guidance of the Holy Spirit, the protection of our guardian angels, to mention only a few of the ways we recognize inner guidance. In psychological terms we speak of guides that come to us in dreams or in active imagination. Yet it seems difficult for us to accept the reality that we have an inner guide whom we can trust, until the awareness of the presence of that guide has been awakened. Recognition of the inner guide seems to come only through experience and a prolonged testing of the wisdom that is spoken. Again, discernment is necessary and, at least at first, the opinion of another trusted person that what the guide speaks is truth.

God speaks to us through our humanness, for that is how he has created us. He speaks to us through our thoughts, our sufferings, our delights, and through all that surrounds us. Whether the communication comes from within or through an external experience, whether the mode he chooses is word, symbol or silence matters little as long as we grasp the meaning. His message may come to us through written or spoken words communicated to us through a book, a letter, or a person. Or the insight may burst upon our consciousness while we are at prayer. A symbol may be weighted with sudden significance. An object in a dream may speak volumes as we learn to decipher its meaning. Even silence may be pregnant with a sense of presence, peace, and meaning as we begin to hear the word of God in it and allow the consequences of that encounter with Truth to transform us. God's ingenuity is infinite.

Learning to understand our own inner language takes us on an individual journey, for the inner voice speaks a unique language that can only be fully understood by the person. It is not a journey made in isolation, for we are led by a loving, personal God who speaks to us in a language he has created us to understand. Embarking on this journey we accept the paradox of arriving at the destination with each step, and of seeing it ever more distant. The numinous moment of encounter with the Divine seems to bring us into contact with the infinite, but that experience is bounded by our finite capacity to experience our God.

2

FROSTED GLASS

It was an ordinary day, hot and dry, not a whisper of a breeze. The shepherd was peacefully tending his father-in-law's flock in the wilderness near Horeb, perhaps thinking how different his life was from the way he used to live in the courts of the Pharaoh, and wondering if he was meant to live out his days as a shepherd. His musings led him nowhere, only helped to pass the time. Then suddenly a bright flame broke the brown monotone of the countryside. Moses was startled, concerned about the safety of his flock, but then he noticed that although the fire came from the center of a bush, the leaves were not burning. Curious, he went closer to look at the strange phenomenon. Then, alone in the wilderness, he heard his name called, "Moses, Moses."

Thereupon Moses and God held a rather lengthy conversation. Moses, incredulous at what God was asking him to do, searched for questions to raise: "I am to go, then, to the sons of Israel and say to them, 'The God of your fathers has sent me to you.' But if they ask me what his name is, what am I to tell them?" God answered simply, "I am who I am." (Ex 3:13–14)

Those words have echoed through the centuries, a revelation of our God: he is who he is, fully himself. In telling us his name God revealed to us another truth: we who are made in his image and likeness are created to be who we are, nothing more, nothing less, no pretense, no falsity. Created in truth, we are called to be true to our Self, and thus to conform to the image of our God. And this message holds yet another facet of truth, that of relationship. The radiance of the solitary bush enveloped in flame, yet not destroyed, shouts the silent lesson of a reality too profound to grasp about our relationship with our God. The energy, the very being of God penetrates all of creation, tenderly holding it in existence, allowing it to be, without consuming it. All that God asks is that the bush be a bush, that the bird be a bird . . . that I be I.

That realization leaves each of us with a question, "Who am I?" We may think we know the answer to that question, but our response too often touches only the surface of our identity, the finite, observable qualities of our person. The seemingly simple task of knowing who we are and of allowing that true Self to emerge is an awesome responsibility. It is so much easier to pretend to be who others think we are, or the person we want others to think we are. We can get so involved in those roles that we come to believe that they define our identity. Then the tragedy is that, thinking that we know who we are, we no longer seek to know. We can unintentionally live our lives in pretense and falsity, without realizing that this is the cause of the vague sense of restlessness and tension that we feel.

There have been times in my life when I have been so caught up in the work I was doing that I found myself assuming the external veneer that went with the position. I would be successful and enjoy my work, but now and then hear an inner prompting which whispered, "This is not who I am." Eventually I would listen to the message and take definite steps to change some aspects of my activities in order to follow the call to be true to my Self. It is a lesson which has been repeated throughout my life. Each time that I listened and responded with action, I came to know a new potential in myself, and caught yet another glimpse of the image of my God within me.

There are many ways of coming to self-knowledge. Sometimes we are brought to face the naked truth of who we are as our persona or external image is stripped away through illness, old age, loss of a job, death of a spouse, or some other suffering. Then only do we realize that our whole concept of who we are is bound up in the roles we play. Others are led to the realization more gradually through the action of God's grace in less painful experiences, or through attentive listening in prayer. The awareness may even come through psychological analysis or counseling. Nonetheless, in whatever way we come to a deeper recognition of our real identity before God, the experience is profound and challenging. Self-knowledge calls us not only to accept our weakness, but to fulfill our potential. It calls us to action.

Several years ago I had a dream in which I saw a rectangular sheet of glass the size and shape of a full length mirror, but the glass was opaque. As I looked at it I heard the words, "Frosted glass is too brittle to live much longer." The dream left a strong impact on me although at first I did not understand its meaning. Then I realized that the mirror shape symbolized the reflection of my true Self which was frosted over by my persona, the roles I was playing, so that I could not see who I really was. The message was clear. Frosted glass, lack of transparency, inauthenticity was too fragile to survive much longer. It was time for it to be shattered so that I might see more clearly who I was. The dream was a preparation for a period of transition which I was entering. I was being called to set aside many good things I had been doing so that I might take a new direction and allow other facets of who I am to develop.

Times of transition in our lives are always opportunities to come to know ourselves better and to live our lives accordingly, following God's desire for us. And they are also times of choice. We are always free to turn away from deeper self-knowledge and continue in our accustomed roles. Most of us turn away many times before we have the courage to shatter the frosted glass and look at the image of our true Self within us. At first the frosted glass serves a positive purpose in our lives, protecting us from the light which we may not be ready to look at. During our early years we must develop a strong ego and, yes, even learn to play the persona roles assigned to us by our family, education and vocation. We refer to this as the need to build our self-esteem and self-concept. It is only when we are secure in some sense of identity that we are ready to look within and gradually learn more of who we really are. Then we are offered the opportunity to allow the protective glass to be shattered, to let go of a persona which is blocking our self-knowledge because it has assumed too much importance. The frosted glass only becomes a negative barrier rather than a protective shield when it is held in place after it has served its purpose. We must be able to use an appropriate persona at times without confusing it with our true identity.

It seems strange that we should find it so threatening to know ourselves and to be who we are created to be. Our hesitancy is an experience of a deep existential dread, the fear of the unknown. We would rather cling to the familiar routines of our lives that give us a sense of security because we think we can control them.

Perhaps our reaction is similar to Moses' experience as he stood before the burning bush. He was frightened, unsure of his ability to speak to the people and lead them, uncertain about standing before the Pharaoh. He knew he could tend sheep and thus provide for his family. God's call meant letting go of his perception of himself as a shepherd, uprooting his family from a simple, but comfortable lifestyle, and walking into the unknown. He did not see anything in himself that was capable of all of this. Yet God was unrelenting, and Moses trusted because he believed.

Knowing who God is and who we are, not just intellectually, but with a loving trust in our relationship, makes us conscious of the awesome responsibility of living our lives in conformity with that truth. We can no longer allow ourselves to be ruled by others' expectations of us or by our own fears. Only by being true to ourselves and to our God do we experience an inner freedom, a peace and joy. And only in this sense of at-oneness within ourselves are we fully free to open ourselves to others and respond to their needs. Our authenticity and transparency allow others to see the

18

God within us. Thus our relationships and our ministry are enriched.

The answer to the question "Who am I?" lies beyond words, beyond symbols, in the silence of knowing that we do not know. God's "I am" is spoken from the depths of eternity, while my "I am" springs from a moment in time. It is an echo of the eternal word. God dwells in me and I in him. In my finiteness I am called to be who I am . . . a person created in the image of God. This is a reality that reaches beyond understanding and can only be glimpsed instant by instant, by those who dare to look.

"Who am I?" is the ultimate question that gives meaning to our lives and direction to our personal journey. The answer matters not so much as the question, for the answer is always beyond our grasp, while the question draws us ever deeper into ourselves and beyond ourselves, into darkness and into light. The darkness of the unknown regions of our inner being is but the blinding flame of God's presence.

Words cannot express the reality of a darkness that is a light, of a knowing that is a not-knowing. To remain on the level of words in expressing this apparent paradox would be futile. The paradox is only reconciled in the unspoken language of the Spirit heard in the depths of our being. It is there that the true Self of each of us listens to the silent word of God. This unspoken communication leads us to a conviction of what we must do, how we must live to conform to our inner truth. That is why it is so important to learn our inner language.

If this whole process is so mysterious, complex, and even incomprehensible, how can we possibly come to know our true Self? The realization of this complexity is an important step on our journey. It leads us to let go of the idea that we can find our way alone, and to turn to God in total dependency and trust. To know who we are is also to see the flame within us and know that it sustains us. This is not a challenge that is beyond our capacity. God is directing our steps so that the journey to know him, to know our true Self, and to be all that he desires us to be is not as difficult as it may sound. We can go forward through alternating periods of darkness and light, confusion and clarity, with the confidence that we are led in safety by a Guide who is our Way, our Truth and our Life.

Coming to know who we really are is a lifelong or perhaps an eternal discovery, for we are created in the image of an infinite God who holds us in existence in an eternal now. We must not fear to ask in prayer, "Lord, who am I?" The response will bring us to both humility and awe. It will call us beyond our human limitations, and bring us into the fullness of our potential.

3

FROGS, LIZARDS AND LEPRECHAUNS

The sudden sound and movement of many small birds fluttering nervously in the trees outside my window broke the morning stillness of the forest. I looked more closely to see what had caused this unusual commotion. It was the first rain of autumn. Gradually the agitation of the birds seemed to change to playfulness as they danced between the drops. It occurred to me then that some of these birds, born in late springtime, had never known the feeling of rain.

That fleeting realization sent a stream of thoughts through my mind, memories of irrational, unnecessary restlessness in my own life that so often stemmed from an experience of the unknown and unfamiliar. There were the times when I worried about the car getting stuck in the mud during a heavy rain; when I dreaded a winter storm, and wondered if a tree would fall on the house; when I was concerned before leaving on a trip about the possibility of a plane crash, or a fire on the cruise ship. The list could go on and on. There are many different degrees of this uneasiness, but they are all connected by the common threads of uncertainty about my future, and a desire to control it. I've learned to call worry, dread, and concern of all types by one name: fear.

These and similar emotions all stem from one root fear that lies deep within us. Our efforts to overcome it only strengthen it. The more we repress it, the more it consumes our consciousness. We simply create different labels for each facet of fear. Is it perhaps in an effort to soften the reality? Is it more acceptable to say that we are worried than to say we are afraid? Or is it simply an effort to describe the varying colors of the emotion? That one elusive, core fear is so difficult to identify because we are afraid to know our fear, yet knowing it is the only way to make friends with it and thus intercept its invasion of our thoughts.

There are so many ways of reacting to fear. Denial is one of the most common reactions because we have been taught that being afraid of anything is a weakness. We not only hide the fear from others, we refuse to admit it to ourselves. Instead we create more acceptable names for fear, hoping that if we do not name it, it will go away. Denying our fear, or pretending we are not afraid, worried or concerned, does not magically dissipate the fear, it only represses it within our unconscious. There it lies, waiting to attach itself to another reality, sometimes so non-threatening in itself that our preoccupation with it puzzles us. Yet we are upset by it. This is the fear that I describe as irrational.

I once had a Latin American teacher on my staff whose usual response to almost anything I said to him was, "Don't worry about that." Although I realized that this was simply an English phrase he used habitually, I would defensively assure him that I was not worried and attempt to clarify what I had meant. All to no avail. My explanation would only evoke another "Don't worry about that." Why was I so concerned about being accused of worrying? It was another aspect of fear that was touched, the fear of being misunderstood. I was not ready to face that fear, so I denied it.

A few years ago I went through what I now refer to as my "fear experience." It was a period of a few months when I became acutely worried about many things, most of which did not deserve such attention. I wondered why I felt such dread, or why I was so worried about small things. It was then that I began to think of these worries as being irrational fears. That, of course, was a step in the right direction, because at first I had refused to admit they had anything to do with fear.

One such experience was my dread of finding frogs in my house. Shortly after moving into an old house in the country, I discovered that I shared the house with frogs. Although I had taught biology at one time, and then felt no reluctance to handling frogs, I soon realized that the possibility of coming upon them in my living space was an entirely different matter. I was apt to find them anywhere: in my bed, on a jar of peanut butter in the cupboard, sitting in the sink waiting for a drop of water. Although I became very adept at catching them, I felt an exaggerated sense of dread as I came home in the evening and searched the house for frogs. How could I live with this uneasiness? I exhausted all outside resources for coping with the situation—Pest Control, the County Agricultural Department, and even the University of California Agricultural Extension Office. No one had ever heard of such a problem. There was nothing that could be done because they knew of nothing that was toxic to frogs. They could only assure me that frogs are good for the garden!

Then, as I came to realize that I must accept this reality, or move out of the house, I gradually faced my fear and entered into the experience. I continued to catch the frogs and put them outside, knowing that they would only find their way back into my space. But most important was my admission to myself that my feelings of dread were real, and neither good nor bad. Then I recognized that I had a choice as to whether to allow them to dominate me or not. Once I confronted the fear and the frogs, the fear no longer controlled me. I was able to free myself of the dread only by accepting the situation as well as my reaction to it. That does not mean that I learned to enjoy the presence of the frogs, or that my feelings of dread disappeared, but only that the circumstance no longer created an exaggerated reaction within me.

The result of accepting an emotion is not that we do not experience it, but that it does not control our actions. When we embrace the emotion as a part of us, it cannot overwhelm us. We are freed from acting simply in response to the feeling. It is as if once we stop trying to destroy it, hold it away from us and struggle against it, its strength is dif-

25

fused. It still exists, but has no power to invade our consciousness and block our rational response.

How does all of this relate to dealing with what might be considered reasonable fear, that is, an emotion that arises from deeper concerns such as fear of losing a job, of serious illness, or of death? I've come to realize that fear by whatever name, triggered by whatever circumstance, imagined or real, is fear. It never deserves to be excused as rational or reasonable. All fear shares a common ground in the psyche. Of course, it is true that some fears spring from our instinctual survival mechanism, such as those that cause us to run away from a tiger, to leave a burning house, or to defend ourselves when attacked. Others are psychological fears of failure, inadequacy, or rejection, while some seem less reasonable, fears of elevators, cats or high places. Nevertheless, all of these fears create in us a desire to protect ourselves and to control our future according to our own perception of what is best for us, so we set up a shield which is meant to isolate us from the experience. The shield is often physical or psychological avoidance.

There is an example of this type of avoidance in the third chapter of Genesis. After Adam and Eve had eaten the forbidden fruit, they experienced fear for the first time. Notice their reaction.

> Then the eyes of both of them were opened and they realized that they were naked. So they sewed fig leaves together to make themselves loincloths. The man and his wife heard the sound of Yahweh God walking in the garden in the cool of the day, and they hid from Yahweh God among the trees of the garden. But Yahweh God called to the man, "Where are you?" he asked. "I heard the sound of you in the garden," he replied. "I was afraid because I was naked, so I hid." (Gn 3, 7–11)

As I read this narrative, I sometimes wonder if Adam and Eve were cast out of the garden not because of their sin of disobedience, but because they allowed themselves to be controlled by their fear, by their lack of loving trust in their God. It occurs to me that if Adam and Eve had stood before their God, acknowledged their weakness, and asked forgiveness, God's response might have been different. Their realization that they had violated their inner truth made them begin pretending to be other than they were, and ashamed to be naked before each other, so they fashioned the protective shield of a fig leaf, the first layer of the persona. The fear that drove them into hiding among the trees in an effort to separate themselves from God shows they no longer felt the trust that springs from intimacy. God had created them in his own image and likeness, and they no longer conformed to that image, to the true Self. That seems more worthy of punishment than a single disobedience.

Theirs was a sin of separation from their inner truth, from each other, and from God. The punishment was even further separation, from the rhythms of nature: Eve would bear children in pain, and Adam would struggle with the land to bring forth food. The fruit of fear is ultimately separation. It can be destroyed only by the union of love. If "love casts out fear," then fear casts out love, and that original fear is still within us, causing us to hide from ourselves, from each other, and from our God. Refusing to accept the root fear, we continue to project it on to objects and circumstances we hope to control.

While it is true that fears come in a variety of sizes and shapes, that some are helpful and some only get in our way, any fear can paralyze us if we do not recognize it and accept it. We must do more than name it; we must embrace it, erasing the separation it has created in us. One of my favorite dreams illustrates this in the language of symbols.

> I am in the living room telling one of my friends a story. She is listening attentively. We decide to go outside as I continue. As we walk through the garden, we notice a small lizard sitting on a low stone fence. My friend is afraid of lizards, but I tell her to go up to it and kiss it.

> She hesitates, but slowly approaches the lizard, bends over and kisses it. The lizard is transformed into a smiling leprechaun, about two feet tall.

Who knows what transformations may take place within us if we approach our fears and kiss them? The lizard sitting on the stone fence of separation symbolizes my alert, wary fears. The little girl in me saw only the frightening lizard until she approached it and kissed it. It was that unifying action that transformed the lizard into a smiling leprechaun, a playful, magical creature.

When I mentioned this dream to a friend, he said it reminded him of the western and eastern ways of knowing described in this anecdote: Two men want to understand a fish. The western man needs to control, so he drops a fishing line into the water, catches a fish, and dissects it. Then he says, "I know fish." The eastern man immerses his head into the water, watches the fish, kisses it, and says, "I know fish." By putting my head into the waters of my unconscious, I observe my fear, kiss it, and know it, thus destroying its power over me.

Yet, even approaching and kissing our fear is not enough if we continue to think of it as something separate from ourselves which we must control. The lizard is within us. We may project it to externals, but the root fear is a part of us. To state it simply, all fear stems from a desire to control which implies separation and domination. If this is true, it follows that to be free from the power of fear in my life I must allow the fear to be, and let go of the desire to eliminate or control it. Paradoxically, that is the only way to transform it into a feeling which energizes rather than paralyzes. Fear is fear. Let it be. In itself it is neither good nor bad. It is only my attitude toward it which makes it a positive or negative force in my life.

Whatever is separated from ourselves because it is not yet loved can be perceived as a threat, and therefore we believe that it must be controlled. Our efforts at "self-control" speak of the division within our very person. It is that division, the basic separation between our conscious ego and our true Self, that spreads out to engulf our relationship with ourselves, with others, and with God. The two great commandments, "Love the Lord your God with your whole Self," and "Love your neighbor as your Self," can never be obeyed as long as our own person is divided, and we are unable to love ourselves. Instead, our ego sets up a protective shield to defend itself from all that is separate.

It is this very isolation that we create which engenders the core fear experienced first by Adam and Eve in the garden. They made a choice which divided their inner unity into opposing desires, and because of this division they began to perceive themselves as separate from God and from all creation. Our fear, too, stems from a deep, personal lack of unity which can infiltrate all of our relationships unless we strike at its roots.

If fear exists only in separation and the consequent need to control, its power can be destroyed only by union and surrender. Just as one basic division within ourselves can engulf all our relationships, so also a total unity within ourselves can encircle all those relationships. To accept and love the true Self is to accept and love God. In Jungian terms, the true Self is the "imago dei" at our deepest center. Acceptance and love imply trust, and fear cannot co-exist with trust. We will still experience the fear of many things, of lizards and tigers, of failure and rejection, of illness, and of death itself, but the emotion will not consume us if we are at-one with our Self and with our God. Union implies love and total, trusting surrender; it negates fear and the need to control.

Jesus himself experienced fear, and we can learn from him how to deal with it. In Mark's gospel we read this account of the hours just before Jesus' arrest:

> They came to a small estate called Gethsemane, and Jesus said to his disciples, "Stay here while I pray." Then

he took Peter and James and John with him. And a sudden fear came over him, and great distress.... And going on a little further he threw himself on the ground and prayed that if it were possible, this hour might pass him by. "Abba (Father)!" he said, "Everything is possible for you. Take this cup away from me. But let it be as you, not I, would have it." (Mk 14:32–37)

"Let it be...." In those words he accepted not only his physical suffering and death, but the human emotions of fear, rejection and humiliation, and surrendered his own desire to shield himself. Perhaps the key words here are acceptance, and surrender. His was not a passive, helpless surrender to what he saw as inevitable, but rather an active, willing acceptance of what was to be. In that stance of acceptance he was freed from the paralysis of fear and able to go out to meet his captors.

We have all read that account of Jesus' struggle with himself the night before his death. We have meditated on his words many times. We often pray, "Thy will be done, on earth as it is in heaven." Why, then, do fear, worry and dread continue to invade our thoughts? Why can't we simply do all we can and then accept what is? Perhaps it is because these realizations remain at the intellectual level and only gradually penetrate to the heart where grace is operative. Knowledge is not enough. Our will must also be involved in the experience. If the fear is to be transformed, it is important that we reach the unconscious level of our psyche where the root fear resides. This is not an impossible task. There are many ways of establishing contact with our unconscious such as:

- praying in a quiet, centered, contemplative mode;
- learning to understand and to listen to our dreams;
- writing dialogues in our journal;
- listening to and expressing our feelings through art forms.

Different methods will serve at different times of our lives. Sometimes the one that seems least likely to help, or most difficult to follow, will be the most productive, and the only way to discover its potential is to experiment. Communication with our unconscious is a way to listen to God, and to open ourselves to receive his strength. I have used all of these techniques at different times and found them to be invaluable tools in my own journey toward inner unity and union with God.

During what I have referred to as my "fear experience" I found that I was able to gain valuable insights through writing dialogues—with fear, with a dream figure, with an inner guide, or with Jesus. The act of writing rather than only fantasizing a dialogue is effective because it slows down the thought process and focuses the attention in a different way than does simply allowing an imaginary conversation to run through our minds. If it is done in a quiet, prayerful way, thoughts that have never occurred to us before may surface because we are truly in touch with the deeper Self. Writing also has the advantage of preserving the words so that we can return to them when we need to be reminded of the truths we heard.

As an illustration of the use of dialogues to get in touch with unconscious feelings, I will share excerpts from dialogues that I wrote in my journal when I was trying to understand and accept the experience of fear. You will notice that the dialogues sometimes move in a halting, repetitive fashion, as if it is taking some time and effort to get to the kernel of the message.

"Fear, I have to talk with you before tonight! Who are you? Why are you projecting on to so many things?"

"Carole, you know who I am. I am your ego fear that all will not go as you desire."

"But my ego is conscious. You are in my unconscious."

"Right, but I am in your personal unconscious. Your ego created me. Remember, I am the opposite of acceptance and surrender. When your ego doesn't want to accept what your Self is doing, she tries to stop it by creating fear. Your ego is not accepting what you are doing! It will lead to her destruction. So, you feel afraid of anything."

"How can I stop being afraid?"

"Accept me."

"What does that mean?"

"If you don't mind being afraid, if you accept being afraid, you cannot be afraid, because acceptance and fear are contrary."

"Is it really that simple? How can I accept you if I don't know who you are?"

"I am fear. I am emotional, irrational and possessive."

"How can I accept the feelings you create in me that are so uncontrollable, and that fill me so?"

"Accept my presence within you, and I will not create those feelings. Know me for what I am, unreasonable and illogical, and I will not bother you."

"I do not really understand all of this, but I do accept the fact that you are irrational, divorced from reality, a trick of my ego. Now, will you please leave me in peace?"

The dialogue seems to proceed in circles, but fear did admit to being illogical. The exercise of confronting my fear and conversing with it objectified the feeling and left me with at least a temporary peace, one step in the right direction.

The next sample dialogue was written a few years later, but also deals with fear and worry. I had been talking with a friend about his fear of illness and pain. The conversation reminded me of a definition of pain that my inner guide had once given me in another dialogue: "Pain is the rejection of feeling." Wondering about the similarity between fear and pain, I pursued the thought, again with my inner guide whom I call Kevin. Here is the dialogue:

"Kevin, it occurred to me today that if it is only in the rejection, non-acceptance of a physical feeling, that it becomes pain, there must be a parallel with fear. Fear seems like the mental counterpart of pain. Is it?"

"Right, Carole, just as pain is the rejection of feeling, worry and fear are both emotions that result from the rejection of not-knowing. I've told you before that you must accept not-knowing. When you do, you will no longer experience worry or fear, because they both stem from wondering what may happen, and wanting to control the happening. Neither worry nor fear arise from the experience of a reality, but rather from wondering if you will be called to experience the reality. If you live in the present moment, and accept not-knowing the future, you will not know worry or fear. They are always projected toward a future reality or situation you do not want to experience. You must let go of your own will so completely that you choose all that Jesus desires for you. Every circumstance of your life brings you to a more intimate union with him if you are united with him in embracing the Father's will. As long as you are struggling to avoid circumstances you do not want to experience, there will be a tension within you that gives rise to worry, dread and fear."

"Kevin, that all makes so much sense, and it is what I wish I could do, yet it is beyond my power. I really feel powerless when it comes to letting go of my own will."

"Carole, you must distinguish between acts of your will and feelings. Letting go of your will and uniting it with God's will, 'fasting from doing your own will,' does not mean you will no longer experience human emotions! Jesus himself experienced fear and dread in the Garden of Gethsemane. You will sometimes be called to submit to physical and mental sufferings. Experiencing pain, worry, fear and other human sufferings does not mean you have not surrendered your will. It simply means you are still on this earth, still human. You will never be totally free from pain, worry or fear. They are part of the human condition. But you must continually strive to purify your desire for what you prefer, and embrace whatever Jesus prefers. Then you will simply notice the pain, worry and fear, and let it pass by, grateful that you are reminded of your weakness."

"Kevin, I'm slowly beginning to grasp what you mean, but still a little confused. If worry is the rejection of not-knowing, and I must accept not-knowing, it sounds like eventually I should not worry. But now you're saying I always will."

"This is what is important: when worry passes through your mind, accept it as you would accept the experience of physical suffering. Notice that it is there. Experience the dread and know that it can lead you closer to God. You know that about physical suffering. Why can't you understand it about mental suffering? Worry, fear and dread, as well as physical pain, can remind you of your dependence on God, your powerlessness, and be a means of grace if you transform them to feelings through acceptance.

"Remember when you realized that it is only through an experience of fear that you can really surrender your will and accept what God wills? You realized that without experiences prayers can seem to be only words. Each time you find yourself in the midst of a

34

situation which brings worry and dread to your mind, you can really surrender and submit to what God wills in a much deeper way than if you are submitting when there is nothing in particular to dread. You need these experiences in order to submit wholeheartedly to God. Otherwise it is like trying to learn to swim without going into the water. As you are ready, you will experience difficulties which allow you to submit to God's will and lovingly embrace it. These times are a special gift. Without them you could not loosen your grasp on your own will. God will not test you beyond your strength, but he will allow these opportunities as you are ready."

As you can see, what comes from the unconscious in these dialogues is not concise and orderly, but emerges in bits and pieces. There are sometimes statements that seem contradictory or inconsistent. At such times it is important to challenge the thought and ask for clarification. It also happens that the content that surfaces in dialogues becomes more focused only in later dialogues. They must be tested as one would test the information given by anyone.

Although dialogues such as these often lack coherence and clarity, they leave you with an intuitive grasp of the truth that you are not yet ready to formulate in logical patterns. Leave them as they are. Later you will find that the thoughts have been integrated into your consciousness, and can be verbalized more easily.

Experiment with dialogues as one way of listening to your inner voice and of learning to know yourself better. Surprises will appear on your paper, and you will be puzzled, startled, dismayed, or overjoyed at what you have written. Also try the other techniques I have mentioned as ways to get in touch with aspects of yourself that lie hidden in the unconscious.

Fear in its many guises is an on-going part of the human

experience, and can be used as a guide to self-knowledge, individuation, and spiritual growth. Since it will often be our companion on our journey, it is wise to learn to recognize it and make friends with it. If we do, it may turn out to be only a mischievous leprechaun.

4

SLOPES AND UPGRADES

I placed another oak log on the glowing embers in the stove. At first I thought it was too late. The log lay there impervious to the heat of the coals. Then gradually its rough edges sparked into flame until the whole log was engulfed in fire. I watched, fascinated, as if I had never before seen a burning log. In a sense, I had not. I had never really been aware of the process by which the dry wood yielded to the power of fire, offering no resistance, being transformed into exquisite, radiant coals penetrated by the fire itself. The log became flame, light and heat, gradually losing its original qualities. But even as I watched and was warmed by the fire, I knew that by morning all that would remain would be cold, grey ashes.

I thought of the grey ash rubbed on my forehead every Ash Wednesday. "Remember, man, that thou art dust and unto dust thou shalt return." Somehow I always dreaded receiving the ashes and walking around all day with a smudge on my forehead, proclaiming to all the world that I had been to Mass. I had been taught that it was to remind me of death, that one day all that would remain of my body would be dust. I always wondered why the priest smeared ashes and not simply dust on my forehead. Suddenly I knew.

It is true that like the oak tree, my body is destined to return to the earth and mingle there with the dust of all creation, but first I am called to approach the burning embers of God's presence within me and allow the fire of his love to penetrate me. It has seemed at times that it is too late, that I have allowed the fire within to die by neglecting it as I was "busy about many things," but then a spark becomes a flame, and I am warmed by the intensity of an awareness of God. Enveloped in love, I feel as if I am transformed for a moment into fire and light. Then, all too soon, all that remains of the experience is cold, grey ash. Yet that very ash is a symbol not of death, but of transformation and resurrection to new life that has taken place. The oak log cannot become ash without yielding to the fire, nor can I. I must repeatedly yield to the experience of approaching the fire of God's presence so that little by little I may be changed. Does it matter that all that remains after such an experience seems to be ash? Beneath the ash the embers still glow, waiting to be stirred into flame.

The phoenix of Egyptian mythology was a bird that consumed itself by fire and rose renewed from its ashes. Everything that is consumed by fire takes on a new form. Perhaps that is why we pray, "Come, Holy Spirit, fill the hearts of thy faithful, and enkindle in them the fire of thy love." It is no wonder that God is described in Scripture as a consuming fire, and by St. John of the Cross as a "living flame of love." In John's poem by that name he describes the mystical experience of transforming union with God in such a way that the reader is drawn at one moment to yearn for the experience, and at the next to draw back as one retreats from the heat of a fire.

That is the human way of approaching God, a few steps forward, and a few steps backward. Is the inexpressible delight of the encounter more than we can sustain? Most of us have not yet reached that stage in our spiritual life. But we often pull back as we realize the change that is taking place within us, or the choice we are called to make and the effect that it will have on our lives. In our weakness we must gradually become accustomed to the experience of God and strengthened to respond to his call. The courage to change is a gift that we are not always ready to receive.

Several years ago, at a time which I now realize was the beginning of a period of radical change in my life, I had this dream:

Jesus is walking in front me on a narrow path. I call out to him. He turns and looks at me. As our eyes meet he says, "There are many who call my name; few who accept the consequences."

I woke up stunned. The vivid quality of the dream left me with a deep sense of immediacy. As the words went through my mind again and again, I knew that this was a moment of choice. I must accept the consequences of calling Jesus' name, of looking into his eyes, or turn and walk away. The choice was mine. With feelings of anticipation and of dread, of excitement and of hesitation, not knowing what the consequences would be, I accepted.

Looking back at that moment now, I am still moved by the memory. A myriad of consequences flash through my mind, both the external changes in my life that are concrete and obvious, and the interior changes, so intangible and impossible to measure or describe. Responding to a call to deeper prayer, I began tentatively to move from an active ministry to a more contemplative lifestyle. I gradually cut back on the amount of time I devoted to professional work in education, and then even changed the focus of my limited active ministry from education to retreat work. This was such a distinct change in my life that I wondered if Jesus could really be asking it of me. Was I only trying to escape into a less hectic pace of life? I was not alone in my uncertainty; my friends also wondered. My religious superiors thought perhaps it was a passing phase, and decided to give me permission to live in solitude for a year "to get it out of my system." It simply did not fit neatly into the pattern of my life, and no one, including myself, could predict where it would lead. I still do not know where it will lead, but I am more comfortable with living in the present and accepting the consequences of calling Jesus' name, whatever they may be. Experience is teaching me to follow where he leads and to trust him. That trust can only grow out of a lived experience of repeatedly yielding to change and discovering that it turns out for the best.

I do not mean to imply that this cluster of changes in my life was clearly understood and straightforward. There were many times of indecision before a choice was made, times of hesitation, of taking a few steps backward before I had the vision or courage to continue to move forward. These were not dramatic moments, but simply a part of the process of change. There are similar moments in everyone's life. Every choice that we make has a consequence that in some way affects us.

When I first thought of "accepting the consequences," I thought only of difficulties and hardships. I thought of "Take up your cross and follow me," forgetting that Jesus also led his apostles to Mount Tabor where he was transfigured before them, and he fixed them breakfast on the shores of the lake after they had spent the night fishing. Maybe I was associating the word "consequences" with the radio program I listened to as a child, "Truth or Consequences." Or I remembered being told that I had to "learn to take the consequences." Now I realize that consequences also include delights.

Of course, consequences flow from every decision we make, and there are many levels of decision in our lives, from the daily decision to get up in the morning in time to get to work, to the more difficult ones we make about getting married, changing jobs, going back to college, or buying a house. But our practice in making the small, daily choices in our lives develops in us the ability to make major decisions. We learn that every choice involves consequences, even though we may not be sure what they will be. A decision does not simply produce a domino reaction of cause and effect in our lives. Consequences are more like the concentric rings of a tree trunk that trace life so slowly that their growth is imperceptible until viewed from the perspective of time.

For example, when I decided to major in Spanish in college, I had no idea what effect this would have on my life, or that it would eventually lead to my teaching in Spain for three years. I realize now that living by myself in an apartment on the Mediterranean, teaching only four hours a day, being without radio or television during those years, opened me to a new experience of prayer that I had not known in convent living where the emphasis at that time was on communal prayer. Who would have predicted that my ability to speak Spanish would result in my entering into contemplative prayer which would eventually evolve into living in solitude? Choices are like stepping stones in our lives, and to go from one to the other sometimes requires a leap of faith. We often cannot imagine the consequences of a choice we make.

Riding on a bus in Boston one day, I was fascinated by the conversation of two women seated behind me. Having just emerged from a seven week Spanish immersion program during which time I had heard no English, I was especially intrigued by their Bostonian accents and their choice of words. They were commiserating with each other about the difficulties in their lives when one asserted with a resigned tone of experience, "Every life has its slopes and upgrades."

It is true, we are sometimes free to linger on the slopes, enjoying the comforts of our lives, and to sit down to rest in the peaceful valleys of pleasant routine, but the time always comes when we know that we must go on. Then a decision must be made. We may choose to try to preserve the status quo and stay in the valley, or to approach the "upgrade." That is a risk. We do not know if we will make it up the mountain, or what lies on the other side. One of the consequences of being human is not knowing the future, and one of the consequences of being Christian is accepting whatever the future may bring. I am not referring only to external events which are beyond our control, but to our call to live out our Christian commitment in the midst of these unexpected events.

The other day I tripped on a crack in the sidewalk and fell, cutting my cheek and fracturing two teeth. I am sure I did not choose to fall, and I am equally certain that God did not decide to knock me down at that particular moment. I simply fell. It was one of those external events over which I had no control, but I did have control over my reaction to the fall. I was free to choose to be angry about the crack in the sidewalk, to be upset about the scar on my face and my broken teeth, or to accept what had happened and be grateful that it was not worse. I chose the latter, not with a Pollyanna attitude, suppressing my real feelings, but with simple acceptance.

In learning to accept the consequences of living as a Christian, most of us trip on the cracks and "fall flat on our face" once in a while. Fortunately we do not all have to experience that literally! We eventually learn that "for those who love God all things work together unto good," and we relax a bit. Until we repeatedly experience the truth of that statement, the words are only words we have heard, but as we struggle to ascend the "upgrades" in our lives and find that the view from the top of the mountain was well worth the effort, the words become conviction.

As we go through life we can be certain of one thing: God is sure to call us to climb mountains, Sinai, Tabor, or Golgotha. Of course, he will also strengthen and refresh us along the way: "In meadows of green grass he lets me lie. To the waters of repose he leads me; there he revives my soul." (Ps 23) Scripture is full of the imagery of mountains and valleys because they poetically portray the human experience.

Reading Scripture can be so much more encouraging than reading the lives of the saints as they used to be written. The biographers seemed intent on purging the saints of all human frailty, leaving them on pedestals high above us. God's word in Scripture is much more realistic. The people of God are shown as struggling, vacillating, and sometimes turning back, yet eventually moving forward. In the Book of

Exodus we read that the Israelites rejoiced at being freed from the slavery of Egypt and regaled Moses as their hero, but when the manna in the desert turned out to be tasteless and they were short on water, they "grumbled against Moses saying, 'Why did you ever make us leave Egypt?' " (Ex 17:3) They had not thought about the consequences of desert travel, and were not ready to accept them.

Even the outspoken Elijah was terrified by the consequences of his actions after he had confronted the priests of Baal, and was therefore threatened by Jezebel. "He was afraid and fled for his life." After a day's journey he came to a wilderness area and "sitting under a furze bush wished he were dead." " 'Yahweh,' he said, 'I've had enough. Take my life.' " Yahweh saw his exhaustion and desperation, and allowed him to sleep for a while. Then an angel served him a scone baked on hot stone, and a jar of water. After eating and drinking, he fell asleep again until the angel woke him and said, "Get up and eat, or the journey will be too long." Strengthened by the rest and food, Elijah started off once again, still running away. After forty days and forty nights he came to yet another mountain, Horeb. There, after surviving wind, earthquake and fire, he heard the sound of a gentle breeze and Yahweh spoke to him as he had spoken to Adam and Eve hiding in the bushes, "What are you doing here, Elijah?" Probably astounded at the question after all he had been through, Elijah responded, "They want to kill me." Yahweh calmly replied, "Go, go back by the same way. . . . " So Elijah, encouraged by the presence of his God, started off again retracing his steps, facing his fear. (1 Kgs 19:1–21)

When Elijah decided to challenge the prophets of Baal, he probably knew he would incur Jezebel's wrath, and he could imagine the sequence of events that would follow. He freely chose that course of action, and still experienced fear that made him run away to save his life. Even after the display of Yahweh's presence and power in consuming the sacrifice when Elijah called on him, Elijah's trust was weak until Yahweh again spoke to him and filled him with strength. Then only could he return to the people and continue his mission. This pattern of strength and weakness, good intentions and failures, courage and fear is so characteristic of our humanness. It should not surprise or discourage us when we too turn back from our resolve now and then.

We are so much like the people we read of in Scripture. We go forward confidently and turn back in fear, only to be reassured by the small, still voice of God within us. Then we continue on our journey, urged on and strengthened by the gentle yet relentless call of our God. One night I dreamed that someone said to me, "Nations of kings and prophets. Look what they do to their prophets." Prophets are not the most popular people, and yet all of us who accept the consequences of following Christ are called to be prophets, so we can be encouraged by the uncertainties and hesitations that colored the determination of the prophets of old.

If we are to accept the consequences of following Christ, we need to be fully aware of them, not before they evolve, but as we stand in their midst. The Spanish philosopher Ortega y Gasset wrote, "Yo soy yo y mi circunstancia." I am I and my circumstances. In other words, I am connected, interrelated with all that surrounds me on an immediate and on a global level. It is impossible to accept those circumstances and the consequences that flow from them, unless I see myself not as standing aside observing them, and therefore sometimes struggling against them in fear, but as being a part of them.

As a child I knew that World War II was a reality, but it was far off and touched my life only minimally. I knew that there was a rationing of gas and of certain food, but my needs were met, so I was in a sense insulated from the effects of the war. Only as I began going to war movies with my friends on Saturday afternoons and entered into the scenario of "Thirty Seconds over Tokyo," "Back to Bataan," and other films, did the reality of the war begin to seem less separate from my world. The 6:00 o'clock news on the radio took on a new, vivid imagery in my mind because I could picture what was happening. The result was fear and nightmares. I would wake up at night imagining Japanese paratroopers crawling through my bedroom window, and dream of bombs striking my house. Needless to say, my mother made me stop going to war movies.

Today we do not have to go to the movies to see the terror and suffering of war-torn nations and starving people. The events of the whole world can be viewed on television in our living rooms, but we can still make an effort to forget the suffering of other people and immerse ourselves in our comfortable routines. The impact of world events seems almost too much to deal with at times. It is easier to turn away and pretend that what happens on another continent really does not concern us. The point is that reality can be psychologically kept at a distance, or it can be recognized as a part of this moment in my world. Only then can I truly live as a Christian at this moment in time.

Much of our difficulty in coming to terms with any level of reality in our lives is due to the incomplete integration of our own person, the imbalance within ourselves. That is why there are so few who can fully accept the consequences of calling Jesus' name. Those consequences include following him through all the realities of our lives, and we can only do that if we are whole enough within ourselves to undertake the journey. Jesus calls our whole Self to follow him, not just one aspect of our person at a time. Yet so often our efforts fail because they are one-sided and out of balance. For example, we throw ourselves, or a part of ourselves, "wholeheartedly" into some form of ministry: visiting convalescent homes, teaching religious education classes, working in the peace movement, or helping with a parish festival, and then wonder why we can't pray, why we are tense and exhausted, or why things are not very peaceful at home. We have equated living out our Christian vocation with expending our energies in doing things to help people. We have forgotten that our whole person must be involved in following Christ, and all the levels of our reality must be taken into account. We cannot truly give of ourselves unless we have a unified Self to give. Sometimes there is a need for healing within ourselves before we can follow Christ as we would like. It can be difficult to admit our need for healing and seek help, but at times it is an essential part of our journey.

When there is a balance and integration within the person, his or her acceptance of and involvement with reality is also balanced and integrated. Whether taking care of a sick child or walking along the beach, working all day or going on retreat, lying in bed sick or shopping for groceries, life is in focus. Then, contrasting experiences, painful, joyful or even tedious, are perceived as balancing points that provide a rhythm in life, rather than as opposing forces that pull us in opposite directions creating tension and exhaustion.

One of the basic consequences of living as a Christian is coming to know ourselves. That entails both struggle and joy. It is a lifetime task that leads to wholeness not only within ourselves but in our perception of all of the reality that surrounds us. It is this integration that makes it possible for us not only to call Jesus' name, but to accept the consequences.

We will be called to submit to fire and be transformed, to climb mountains and to relax in the cool valley by a refreshing stream. The slopes and the upgrades of our lives will alternate, but we will have the constant reassurance of following one who loves us and knows how to set the pace.

5

THE PARENTHESIS

As I walk along the narrow, dirt road through the forest, snatches of the morning news skip through my mind, fracturing the tranquil moments. I let each thought slip by, hoping it will not return, only to meet it at the next step: the lack of fall rain points to a danger of drought, while forecasts of excessive spring rain predict possible flooding; the position of the sun, moon and earth, along with the restless activity of cats and dogs, suggests the probability of an earthquake during the next week. Record keeping, forecasting and modern technology make predictions about everything from the weather and the rise and fall of the stock market to the possibility of nuclear war the material for casual conversation. Parents are told of the sex of their unborn baby; the terminally ill are informed how many days, weeks, or months they have to live. Focusing on the present moment becomes a challenge rather than a natural way of living. We are continually projected into the future and filled with hope, anticipation and fear—a strange mixture. We seem to have an insatiable need to develop technology which enables us to predict and thereby control future events.

The irony is that reaching for reassurances that will calm our concerns often only unearths predictions that feed our fears. We are caught up in a ceaseless effort to insulate ourselves from the unpleasant realities that may come into our lives.

Suddenly a bevy of quail reluctantly takes to flight as I disturb its browsing through the woods. The rush of wings brings me back to the beauty of the present time and space that envelop me and I again relish the gift of the moment, letting go of past and future thoughts.

The paradox which is apparent in these musings is that

the ability to remember and reflect on the past and to anticipate and imagine the future is also a gift, a unique quality of our humanity that is not shared by other creatures. Yet it is a gift which must be held in careful balance. Memories and expectations are meant to enhance the present, but all too often we allow them to destroy it by invading and overwhelming our capacity to savor the instant in which we live.

We have all listened to people who live in the past repeatedly recounting the same events, or wishing the "good old days" would return. Perhaps we have spent some time there ourselves when life was especially difficult. It is also tempting to dwell on a hurt, a rejection or a loss, to spend sleepless nights wondering if we said the right thing or made the right decision in a certain situation. We even spend idle moments wishing for a repetition of an idyllic period in our lives and trying to re-create it in our imaginations. Then too, we so often cling to a persona that has served us well for the past ten years, hesitating to let go of it and be who we are now, at this time of our lives. It was a safe and secure image that we used to convince others and ourselves of our abilities. In the past the role we played was authentic, but now it is no longer appropriate. It is pretense.

While it is true that brief excursions into our memories can give us the courage to continue our journey, extended sojourns can dull our ability to perceive the present circumstances from the stance of faith. The past has the power either to sharpen or to cloud our vision. The choice is ours to allow our memories to become an escape or even a burden, or to allow them to provide a support and an environment in which we are strengthened to embrace the present reality of our lives. Remembering the past and planning for the future need not take us away from the present, but dwelling in the past and worrying or fantasizing about the future can consume the present and destroy our awareness of its amazing possibilities.

The ability to look toward the future is also a gift which must be carefully used. It can be like the experience of riding on an escalator. We can focus all our attention on the crucial, final step when we must stand poised and ready to step onto the level floor, or we can notice the smooth, effortless movement and enjoy the ride, relaxed in the realization that when the appropriate moment comes we will step with ease into the future space.

Our lives are enriched by our ability to prepare for what the future holds and even to mold its shape. We can build shelters and install heaters and air conditioners to create comfortable environments, exercise, eat well and take vitamins to stay healthy, study to prepare for a desired profession, save money for a long-awaited trip to Europe. The possibilities are endless.

On the other hand, we can sit back and worry about tomorrow, imagining the worst that may happen. Some of us have a particular talent for doing that. We find ourselves conjecturing about the future to the point that "what if . . . " becomes a recurring phrase in our thoughts. Then the future controls our perception of the present.

· The instant in which we live stands enclosed between the arms of the parenthesis of past and future, arms which can imprison or embrace.

The time between the crucifixion and the resurrection of Jesus must have seemed like a confining parenthesis in the lives of those who loved him, one filled with doubt and fear. At the last supper Jesus had told them, "In a little while you will not see me. . . . You will look for me. . . . I will come back to you. . . . I am going away and I shall return." (Jn 14) These words made no sense to them in the light of what had happened. The terrible experience of Jesus' arrest and crucifixion did not fit into their understanding of his comment that he would be away for a little while. Their world, their dreams were shattered. All that they had hoped for as his popularity grew, the kingdom and the status they had envisioned, now seemed to be completely destroyed. They wondered how they would pick up the pieces of their lives. What did the future hold? Would they too be arrested and put to death? They were paralyzed, held captive inside the parenthesis of the past and the future.

There are times when we find ourselves in a similar parenthesis. The future that had filled our dreams and plans is suddenly closed to us. We are imprisoned in a present that seems hopeless. One devastating moment is all it takes to change our vision of the future and fill us with dread. It may be a crippling accident, the death of our child, a routine medical examination that reveals an incurable disease. Only as we gradually and painfully adjust to the new reality do we realize that our plans had been based on our independence and ability to achieve what we set out to do. We are called to accept our dependence and powerlessness, and turn with more mature hope to our God who carefully holds us in his hands and breathes new life and strength into our hearts.

That acceptance will open the parenthesis and a new future will stretch out before us. It will not be the future we had envisioned, but one in which we are grateful for each moment of life. The present becomes a precious gift to be treasured. We are freed from being dominated and held captive by the future.

So often when we are plunged into the present moment by an intense experience of joy, fear or tragedy, it grasps our whole attention so that at least for a time the past and future seem not to exist. But that intensity is short-lived. We soon return to a consciousness of where we are, standing poised on the last step of the escalator. At this point it is a deep underlying hope that gives us courage.

Then we remember that Jesus has kept his promise and has returned to dwell within us. We live and breathe in the vibrancy of his creative presence. His infinite love holds us in existence and frees us to live in the eternal present moment. But the choice is always ours to perceive the parenthesis as imprisoning or embracing us. It is the hope which Jesus gives us that transforms the arms of the past and future from a prison into a loving, supporting embrace.

Hope is central to an authentic acceptance of the present. It emerges out of remembrances of past experiences and is directed toward future fulfillment. A familiar ejaculation reminds us that "Divine Providence has helped; Divine Providence can help; Divine Providence will help." Remembrance of God's loving care in the past reassures us that it is constant. Hope gives meaning to the present and clothes it in trust. Although it is one of the theological virtues with which we are gifted at baptism, it can lie dormant if it is not nourished. How do we strengthen our hope? By hoping and discovering that our hope is not in vain.

It is hope that creates in us the capacity to accept, to trust and to wait even as we make plans and move toward the future.

We can resist waiting in the present and struggle against it. We resent our powerlessness to escape from our limitations and the circumstances which imprison us, not realizing that our very resistance transforms the waiting into quicksand which pulls us ever deeper into its morass. Only graced experience can teach us how to wait calmly so that we will be free to step into the future when the time is right. That experience is the nourishing soil of our hope. Experience and faith give us reason to trust and to hope.

Waiting is part of living that is woven into the fabric of time. But there are so many ways to wait. Doctors provide waiting rooms in which we sit distractedly paging through magazines. Designers of airport terminals know we will spend money to entertain ourselves and make our wait more bearable, so they provide cocktail lounges, newsstands and gift shops. We try to occupy our minds to escape an awareness of the present and thus "make the time pass more quickly." We can so lose the art of drawing upon what is within us that we must depend on external stimuli. Then we crave doing and flee from the parenthetical moments when we can simply be alone with our thoughts . . . and with our God.

This is a common tendency in contemporary society.

Some people have a real fear of being alone with nothing to do. Their inability to savor the present creates a time of waiting which is focused on the future. The present then seems like a void which must be filled at all costs with distractions. In reality, it is more like a priceless gift which we must unwrap if we are to thrill in its beauty. If we have the courage to unwrap the present, we find an exquisite jewel.

This realization struck me forcefully one day when I was living in Spain. The incident is imprinted vividly on my memory. I went to the train station in the small town where I lived to catch a commuter train into Barcelona. I found that I had just missed the train and had to wait an hour for the next one. I sat down in the empty waiting room with nothing to do. An extraordinary thing happened: for the first time in my life I did not mind waiting. In fact, it did not seem like waiting. I was able to enjoy being present to myself and to God. The hour was more like an opportunity than an inconvenience. Looking back at that experience I realize that my lifestyle and general pace of life in Spain had relaxed me and opened me to living in the present. When I returned to California, I resolved to preserve that less hectic stance toward life, but I soon got caught up in the race with time. It is only in recent years that I have been able to recover the ability to savor the present moment again, most of the time.

Times of waiting in our lives, whether they be short intervals of waiting for a bus, or longer periods of waiting for an illness to pass, can be opportunities rather than interruptions. But this requires hope which releases us from being entangled in desire for our own pleasure and enables us to find our rest in God. A period of painful waiting filled with worry, depression or suffering can seem like a long, dark tunnel. It is hope which allows us to fix our gaze on the light at the end and continue walking. Just this morning I heard of families who had been evacuated from their expensive homes because of a forest fire. While they awaited news all they were told was that sixty homes had been destroyed and the fire still raged. Each family wondered if its home had been spared. There is no way to avoid the suffering of such waiting, but acceptance of the circumstances in faith and hope can open us to receive the grace and strength that we so desperately need.

The time between the ascension of Jesus and the descent of his Holy Spirit upon the disciples was a period filled with terrible uncertainties about what was going to happen. Jesus had told them only "not to leave Jerusalem, but to wait there for what the Father had promised." He added, "John baptized with water but you, not many days from now, will be baptized with the Holy Spirit." (Acts 1:4–5) They had no idea what this meant, but after Jesus left them on the Mount of Olives they returned to Jerusalem and gathered together in the upper room to wait, joining in continuous prayer. They were frightened and did not know what was going to happen or what the future held. Should they return to their fishing boats and pick up their lives where they had left them? They were followers with no one to follow. It was only their hope and faith in Jesus' promise that held them there and prepared them to receive his Spirit. Their waiting became an opportunity for prayer and their lives were moved in a new direction. This is the potential of the present moment, even when it is filled with uncertainty and fear.

One of the darkest and most unusual times of waiting that has ever been described must be the three days that Jonah spent sitting in the belly of the whale. Plunged into a seemingly hopeless situation, he probably did not pass the time reflecting on the opportunity offered him by the present moment. Yet it proved to be a fruitful experience. Perhaps reviewing the chain of events which led to his desperate state will help us to understand his reaction and see a parallel with our own ways of dealing with time.

It all began with that fateful moment when Yahweh spoke to Jonah telling him rather forcefully, "Up! Go to Nineveh, the great city, and inform them that their wickedness has become known to me." (Jon 1:1) Jonah was a rather ordinary man and could not imagine himself walking through the streets of Nineveh confronting the people with their sinfulness, so, unable to accept the possibility that Yahweh would help him and protect him, he decided to flee from the present challenge. He tried to avoid facing reality by taking a ship for Tarshish, a distant port in Spain. Once on the ship he escaped even further by descending into the hold and falling fast asleep, taking refuge in his unconscious world so effectively that he was unaware of the raging storm. But it was all to no avail. He was jolted back into the real world of the present moment by frightened sailors telling him to call on his God to calm the storm, the very God from whom he was running away. Jonah admitted that Yahweh's anger with him was probably the cause of the violent storm and told the sailors to throw him into the sea to calm the waters. He knew this would be the end of his life. The sailors waited until there was no more hope of saving the ship and then, asking Yahweh's pardon, threw Jonah overboard. The sea grew calm immediately.

The most violent storm was actually within Jonah himself. He had refused to accept the grace of the present moment and follow the call of his God. Instead he had used every avoidance technique that came to mind. Once he came to terms with that refusal and accepted responsibility for his action, Yahweh gave him safe refuge and a precious gift of time to reconsider. He sent a large fish to swallow him. Of course, the environment of the belly of the whale was not the ideal waiting room: there were no magazines to peruse. Nor was it a tranquil spot Jonah would have chosen for a period of quiet meditation. Nevertheless, it served the purpose. There was no way Jonah could escape. He was left alone with his thoughts and his God. Gradually his faith in Yahweh fanned the dying embers of hope into flame, and he turned to prayer.

Unpleasant parentheses in our lives are like times spent in the belly of a whale. They do not occur at the time and place we would choose. It is in setting aside our own preferences and accepting our powerlessness that we are able to hear what God is saying to us. As Jonah was stripped of all control over the externals of his life, he was at last free to see himself as he really was. His prayer reveals his journey into the depths of his inner self. "I went down into the countries underneath the earth, to the peoples of the past." Then he was able to say, "The vow I have made, I will fulfill." (Jon 2:7, 10). When Jonah reached that moment of commitment, he was able to embrace the reality of the present moment with new faith and hope. He then found himself once again on the shore, standing in the light of a new level of consciousness, aware of his own helplessness and of Yahweh's mercy and power.

With this new awareness, Jonah was able to walk into Nineveh and speak the word of Yahweh, living each present moment and not fearing the future. Of course, as the story unfolds we see that Jonah had not completely learned his lesson. When the people of Nineveh repented and Yahweh spared the city, Jonah became angry with his God. Caught up in his new role as prophet, he expected his prophecies to come true. The story ends with Jonah pouting under a withered castor-oil plant, imprisoned once again in the arms of yet another parenthesis, wishing he had acted differently in the past and wondering what the future would bring.

Time after time, with infinite love and patience our God focuses our attention on the exquisite gift of the present that we might gradually learn to appreciate its potential. But when the moment is clouded over with regrets or worries, it is difficult to see its beauty. We must be content to wait.

Waiting is a theme that often surfaces in dreams because it is an integral part of human experience. The dream message can strengthen us to cope with the waiting and not try to avoid its lesson. In the following dream the message was clarified by the symbols of the square table, the upstairs room and the black circle on the floor.

I am in a room with another woman. The room is empty except for a square table. The woman says, "Take off

59

your clothes. Go upstairs to another room. There you will see a small black circle on the floor. Stand on it until someone tells you what to do."

As I worked on the dream, I understood that the square table and the circle were both symbols of wholeness. The first symbolized work that was completed, and the second represented my center, or Self. The circle is also a symbol of femininity and receptivity. My clothes were the persona that had become a part of my identity. I was being told to leave behind the work I had finished and the roles I had filled, and to go upstairs to a more spiritual level. There I was to remain in my center, attentive as I waited for a message. The color black often symbolizes the unknown or the unconscious, an appropriate color for a space of waiting.

To wait is to live in expectation. Hope and faith make waiting possible; love gives it meaning. It is love that has the power to transform us and thus to change our perception of the present moment. A time of waiting in itself is neither pleasant nor unpleasant. It is our way of dealing with it that colors it, that fills it with darkness or light.

The experience of Jonah in the belly of the whale and of the disciples in the upper room after the ascension demonstrates the potential of a parenthesis in our lives. Both were times of transformation: Jonah courageously went to Nineveh to preach repentance, and the disciples descended from the upper room to proclaim the resurrection of Jesus. If our times of waiting are spent standing within our own interior circle of attentiveness to the present moment, we too will hear the message God is speaking to us and receive the strength of his Word. Whether these are periods of excited anticipation, of loneliness or of suffering, the challenge is the same: to accept the grace of the present.

Heaven is described as being an eternal now, an eternal present moment. There are no escalators in heaven to project us toward an unknown future. We will rest in an awareness of what is. Perhaps life is given to us as a time of apprenticeship to learn to exist in the present now. While we are here on earth we must depend on faith and hope to help us accept each instant and not allow the past or the future to control our actions. That was the empowering lesson that the disciples and Jonah learned. It freed them to be themselves and to respond to what God was asking of them.

That freedom is the only atmosphere in which we can truly live our lives as Christians. It is the freedom of the children of God. Without it we are imprisoned by fears and unable to develop to spiritual maturity.

As we watch the evening news on television and hear of tragedies, wars, disasters and terrorism, or as a period of uncertainty and suffering enters our own lives, it is tempting to want to escape into the hold of the ship, our own little world, and go to sleep. But that is not the solution, for we know that we will awaken to the real world again. The challenge of each moment is to realize its potential and remain in continuous prayer as the disciples did. Then we will receive the Holy Spirit and go forth to live our lives in joyful freedom ready to follow God's call. Every parenthesis in our lives will be God's loving embrace.

6
DANDELIONS

"Attention all Dandelions, please meet on the terrace at 1:30." This became a familiar announcement on the high school P.A. system. It started rather unintentionally.

When we introduced a series of non-credit enrichment courses, I developed a course designed simply to enhance the students' sensitivity to the beauty of the ordinary things that surround us everyday. We focused on each of the five senses, noticing the rhythmic sounds of a lawn sprinkler, the variety of patterns on front doors, the shapes and spaces created by telephone wires cutting through the sky, the textured roughness of a rock, the velvety soft surface of a leaf, the fragrance of an apple or a new tennis ball, the sharp flavor of a piece of rye bread. Because the term sensitivity was often misused and misunderstood in the late sixties, I changed the title from "Sensitivity to Beauty" to "Orientation to Dandelions," those frequently overlooked gems of symmetry and color that we call weeds and nonchalantly trample underfoot. It was the students who began calling themselves Dandelions, delighting in tantalizing their friends by creating an aura of secrecy about the class. But since that time dandelions have had a special meaning in my life.

So often we fail to take the time to notice the familiar things in our environment, closing ourselves off from the surprises that lie waiting for us. This is true not only in the external world of the senses, but in our inner world. There too, exquisitely formed dandelions are overlooked or discarded as weeds. They are the options in our lives that we either fail to notice or perceive as disruptive of the orderly, well groomed lawns of our life-plan. Options present themselves in the realms of both actions, choices we must make about what to do, and attitudes, inner mind-sets that influence our feelings, emotions, and consequent stance toward life.

One reason we do not always recognize options that surround us is that our culture and training attune us only to a certain wave length which limits our perception of reality. The value system inherent in a culture colors our view of that reality. Unless we consciously strive to break through the boundaries of our experience and open ourselves to new ways of perceiving our outer and inner worlds, we are not free to notice our options, whether they be of actions or attitudes.

Our experience of options or choices in our life often falls into one of two categories:

(1) There are none.
(2) There are too many.

In the first case we find ourselves on a dead-end street with no place to turn and no way out of an unpleasant situation or emotion. We have a job that we hate, but feel trapped because we can find no alternative. We're caught in a traffic jam on our way to the airport and our level of anxiety is rising. We are depressed, do not have any enthusiasm for anything, and cannot lift ourselves out of that state of inertia. We are told that we have an incurable disease and are filled with a sense of helplessness. One of our children is using drugs, but we can find no way to prevent it.

I once heard of a hospital located at the end of a dead-end street called in Spanish "Salsipuedes Street." Broken up into three words, that translates as "Leave If You Can Street." That expresses well the frustration and challenge we face when we feel that there are no options. There are always options available to us, but for various reasons we do not perceive them.

Sometimes we are not aware of possible choices that we have because they are outside the framework of our cultural values and our experience. That is, they are apparently unacceptable, so we refuse to consider them. For example, we may meet a friend who obviously wants to talk about a problem she has, but we rush off saying, "I'm sorry I can't talk with you now because I would be late for an appointment." In the United States we place a high value on punctuality which can overrule our concern for other people. In other cultures being on time is not given such high priority. Values such as efficiency, success, and reputation can easily blind us to the importance of kindness, availability to others, and simply being ourselves.

This could have been the case with the Roman centurion who came to ask Jesus to cure his servant who was paralyzed and in great pain (Mt 8:5–13). Most men of that culture and time would not have thought of asking a controversial Jewish man to perform a miracle. Had someone suggested it to them, they would have laughed. But this Roman was different. He was able to step out of the boundaries of his cultural bias and notice a possibility.

Our cultural boundaries consist not only of our ethnic culture, but also of the sub-culture to which we belong. Secretaries, lawyers, waitresses, teachers, mothers, priests, nurses, religious, students, etc. form sub-cultures, each with its own set of values and expected behaviors. We are trained in what it is proper for a person in each group to do, and we hesitate to look at an option which might be considered unusual because "it has never been done before." A young doctor would not want his patients to see him working at a gas station on weekends to support his family even though he was having difficulty getting his practice started and paying off his debts. That activity does not appear on the list of expected behavior guaranteed to inspire confidence in patients. Attitudes and values are so deeply embedded in cultures and sub-cultures that we are unaware of them and unwittingly allow them to control our decisions.

Several times in my life I have been able to pursue new and exciting directions by exploring the possibility of doing something that had never been done before by a member of the sub-culture of my religious community. At a time when few of our sisters were working outside of our own schools or hospitals, or living alone, I asked to accept a position as a Spanish teacher in an American school in Spain. I was amazed when the permission was granted. Later I felt called to live in solitude as a hermit. This was another departure from the usual pattern of my religious community which focuses on active ministry. Again, my request was granted. There have been other times when I did not pursue a possibility because it seemed out of the question. We can sometimes fail to perceive something as an option simply because it is outside the realm of norms within which we think we must act.

In other situations it seems we have no choices because those that come to mind are too risky. We discard them immediately. We refuse to accept a new kind of work because we may not succeed. We avoid seriously following a call to deeper prayer because "God may ask something of me that I can't do. I don't have the courage to listen to him." Often possibilities that seem too frightening are blocked from our consciousness and not even thought of as options.

This kind of fear could have prevented the woman in the gospel from reaching out to touch the fringe of Jesus' cloak hoping to be cured (Mt 9:20–22). She must have wondered what might happen if her boldness were discovered, but that did not prevent her from choosing that course of action. The men who lowered their friend through a hole in the roof in order that he might gain access to Jesus were certainly taking a chance, but that did not stop them from seeing the possibility (Lk 4:17–25). Too often when a risk-laden choice lies before us our ego distraction mechanism automatically goes into play and we prevent the thought from being considered, pushing it back into our unconscious mind.

Then too, there are options that we miss simply because they are too obvious, like the dandelions in the lawn. Someone who is handicapped by an accident is told, "You're just going to have to learn to live with this." That, of course, is rejected as a truism. It is obvious that the person will have to live with the handicap. What is not discerned is that the learning process does include options. A limitation of any kind, whether it be physical, economic or situational, can open new doors. There is always a flip-side to what appears negative that is hidden from our view because we fail to turn over the coin and look at the other side. So often it is only in looking back over the years that we can realize this truth. How many times what seemed to be a distressing situation opened the way to a marvelous opportunity.

I remember the time I was told I would have to move from my hermitage in the country because the house was going to be torn down. I was initially very upset, but as a result of being forced to look for options, I found a more suitable hermitage in a beautiful setting. Another example of a negative situation which opened the way to something new was the lack of a piano I could play in the small Spanish town where I lived. That led me to study classical guitar which I still enjoy. Years later learning of a serious illness seemed devastating at first, but led me to deeper self-knowledge, spiritual growth, and greater understanding of others with similar problems. The options in this case were on the attitudinal level. There was no way I could prevent the illness, but there were various ways of dealing with it.

In summary, we frequently think we have no options in a given situation because they are hidden from our view. This may be for one of the following reasons:

(1) our cultural values indicate that some choices are unacceptable;
(2) fear of failure makes some decisions appear too risky;
(3) the possibilities before us are so simple and obvious that we fail to notice them.

There are always options before us, but they are not always easy to see until we look with the eyes of faith and hope. Our memory of God's loving care of us serves to sharpen our vision and to enable us to see the way out of the dead-end street, or to notice the flip-side of the coin. What appears to be a black hole can actually be an opening to a new path.

I recently had a dream that provided me with a realization of this truth through a vivid image:

> I am following a woman along a narrow path beside a stream. The path enters a dark tunnel but she continues. I hesitate to follow because I see no light at the end of the tunnel and because I notice the ground is muddy. I remember that I forgot to change to my walking shoes and have on my new shoes. I tell her I will walk above the tunnel and meet her at the end. Then I turn around. She comes with me. As we re-enter the bright sunlight I see a beautiful, wide stream running parallel to the tunnel. This stream has colorful flowers growing along its banks. We decide to follow that stream.

In the dream the conscious ego, myself, had not seen the other lovely stream which we could easily follow. I saw only the path in front of me and allowed myself to be led by a part of my unconscious, a shadow figure which may have represented a value or an emotion which was blinding me to the presence of another path. Once I took charge of the situation by refusing to walk into the dark, I was freed to look around me and perceive another way to proceed. The message of the dream was that I must not allow myself to be led blindly by unconscious forces, but must have the courage to take the initiative to explore other paths in the light of consciousness. The dream was also reassuring because it showed me that there was another option which I could choose in the situation in which I found myself in my conscious life.

At the other extreme, rather than seeing no options before us, we are sometimes overwhelmed by so many that we are paralyzed and unable to make a choice. It is like standing before a closet full of clothes and saying, "I don't have a thing to wear." Overload shuts down the system and produces inertia. At the simple everyday level we may find that we have so much to do that we spend our time deciding what to do first and the day slips by. Or a student may find he or she is interested in so many college majors that he or she spends years sampling courses and becomes known as a perpetual student who cannot get on with life.

One problem in considering multiple options can be that we sort them out only on the rational level, failing to listen to our inner voice which offers us guidance. We look at the lawn full of dandelions and do not know which one to pull out first, so, feeling powerless to begin, we do nothing. The inner voice may suggest that we dig up just one each day, or that we simply learn to enjoy their beauty. Those are not rational solutions, but they will bring us peace of mind. At least we have made a decision to begin to take action. "Keep watching the wind and you will never sow, stare at the clouds and you will never reap." (Eccl 12:4)

The obvious question at this point is "How do I discover the hidden options in my life, or how do I make a choice when a variety of possible actions or attitudes is available?" Unfortunately, there is no clear-cut answer to that question, no checklist of "steps in making a decision." There are, however, some ways of setting up optimum conditions which provide the milieu for making choices.

First, it is important to relax. The panic and tension that grip us when an important choice must be made can result in tunnel vision which makes it impossible for us to see the beautiful, sunlit stream that runs parallel to the tunnel. We see only that which lies directly before us and blindly follow our first inclination.

This tension distorts our perception of the situation. In order to gain perspective and perceive the reality which is before us we sometimes need to take a step backward and not rush to a decision. The proper perspective allows us to put things in balance, to notice their relative size and importance in the landscape of our lives. "To perceive" is derived from a Latin word meaning "to seize wholly" or "to see all the way through." That is the challenge we face when making an important choice: to put the options in perspective and grasp their reality.

This is more easily said than done. We usually need the assistance of both outer and inner guides. We are so used to talking things over with someone, or seeking advice in other external ways, but we sometimes miss inspirations that come to us subtly through a chance remark that we overhear or an advertisement in the newspaper. If we are open to these messages, we can be led to investigate options we might otherwise have overlooked.

Most of us are even less in tune with listening to our inner guides. The solution to a problem often comes at an unexpected moment in prayer, or in a dream. Of course, the dream message is almost always cloaked in imagery because that is the language of the unconscious. But if we learn how to decode the dream symbols, a reservoir of guidance is available to us.

Remember the story of the Egyptian pharaoh who was afraid that the number of Israelites in his realm might become a threat to his power? He issued a command, "Throw all the boys born to the Hebrews into the river, but let all the girls live." (Ex 1:22) One Israelite woman refused to believe that there were no options available, no ways to save her child. She must have been filled with dread and paralyzed with fear at first, picturing her baby drowning in the river, but she managed to hide him for three months while considering what to do. That gave her time to gain perspective and perceive a possibility, one filled with risk. She must have sought advice from her husband and friends, and she might even have had a dream which indicated a plan of action. Being a devout Israelite she certainly prayed to Yahweh for inspiration.

A creative plan finally came to her mind, one that others must have warned her was ridiculous. Yet something had convinced her that this was worth trying, perhaps her faith in the inner voice which she heard. "When she could hide him no longer, she got a papyrus basket for him; coating it with bitumen and pitch, she put the child inside and laid it among the reeds at the river's edge." (Ex 2:3-4) She then had her daughter watch from a hiding place so that when the pharaoh's daughter appeared and found the baby the young girl could offer to find a Hebrew woman to nurse the baby. Amazingly the plan, outrageous by all human standards, worked. The woman was able to raise her own child and then took him to the pharaoh's daughter who treated him like a son and named him Moses.

The story provides a mini-lesson in choosing among options. Moses' mother could have given in to the apparently inevitable fact that her son was to be killed. There seemed to be no options that were acceptable. The pharaoh's daughter might have been obedient to her father and thrown the baby into the river. And even if that did not happen, what Jewish mother would want her son raised as an Egyptian? But she took the time to listen to her inner voice and then had the faith to follow that inspiration.

Most of the time the options set before us do not involve life or death decisions, but often they can change the direction of our lives. We have been given the gift of free will and with it the responsibility to choose. "He has set fire and water before you; put out your hand to whichever you prefer." (Sir 15:16) We are so fearful that we may make the wrong choice and touch fire. That is possible, but if we make our decisions carefully, taking time to perceive the reality that lies before us and listening to our inner and outer guides, we can trust that we will be given wisdom.

> ... if your plea is for clear perception,
> if you cry out for discernment,
> if you look for it as if it were silver,
> and search for it as for buried treasure,
> you will then understand what the fear of Yahweh is,

73

and discover the knowledge of God.
For Yahweh himself is the giver of wisdom,
from his mouth issue knowledge and discernment.
  (Prv 2:3–6)

The wisdom to know how to delight in the dandelions in our lives is a gift that lies within us. We have only to open our eyes to their beauty. Then they are transformed from weeds to cups of sunlight that bring us joy. Options in our lives are also gift. Perception and wisdom allow us to reach out and pick the right one. We have only to listen and we will be led.

7

THE MERRY-GO-ROUND

With serious deliberation, I carefully picked out a blue and green, ornately decorated wooden horse with a golden mane, and climbed on top of it, settling myself firmly in the saddle and clutching the brass pole. Then the magic began as the music started to play, the merry-go-round began to turn and the horse moved rhythmically up and down. I felt as if I were flying! My excitement mounted as I approached the brass ring and reached out to hook it with my finger, hoping my horse would cooperate by moving up to put me in a better position. I did it! The ring was in my hand and now the challenge was to toss it into the smiling mouth of the wooden clown face. I failed, but there was another chance, and another, and another, as the merry-go-round returned me again and again to a brass ring. It made little difference to me that no prize was offered for my efforts. The momentary thrill of occasional success was enough to entice me to keep reaching and tossing.

Going through my mail this morning was something like that ride on the merry-go-round. Tantalizing brass rings appeared again and again, each offering me one more chance to satisfy a craving. First there was the familiar sweepstakes envelope. My curiosity led me to look inside and read that I had another opportunity to win ten million dollars, or at least the house of my dreams, a luxury yacht, or a Mercedes Benz! Without too much struggle, I decided not to reach out for that brass ring, only to find myself confronted by another, a catalogue of books and records. That was more tempting. I spent some time browsing through the pages of gift ideas, discovering much that I had not realized I wanted. Common sense and lack of money won out and I put that temptation aside. I then picked up the new issue of *Time* magazine and opened it to see what the major events of the week had been. Yes, there too were pages of almost irresistible brass rings waiting to be grasped: new cars, diamonds, computers, even a typewriter "that turns a boring writer into a born writer," as well as machines that would make it possible for me "to take a longer lunch." It seemed there were as many pages of colorful advertisements as news stories. The one that really caught my attention was for a new credit card that provided a year-end summary of charges which would "get my life in order." Was it really that easy to get my life in order? With that incredible offer in mind, I put aside the magazine and went on to my real mail.

The motivation behind all of these brass rings is that someone wants to make money so he or she can buy the luxury yacht, the new car, or the diamond. The only way that can be achieved is by convincing other people that they should spend money, so it becomes a vicious circle. Our consumer culture rides on that merry-go-round which creates a spinning sensation that leads some to shout, "Stop the world, I want to get off!" But is that drastic reaction really the answer? There must be a way to learn to enjoy catching the brass rings and tossing them into the clown's mouth once in a while just for fun, without allowing myself to be caught up in the never ending search for one more thing, one more luxury item, one more convenience that will satisfy me.

Madison Avenue has mastered the art of enticement, of creating desires in me that I never knew existed. I often do not even know that I want something until I see a commercial on television or notice an advertisement in a magazine. Then I begin to think, "That would really help me get my work done more efficiently," or "It's time my family had a vacation in Hawaii, and this is a good buy." The seeds of desire are planted in me, but they can grow only if I encourage them. What I do with those seeds is up to me. I experience desire and I alone have the freedom to choose

78

how to react to it. No one has the power to control my choices.

We humans enjoy the capacity to want something, even to wish for it and to dream of having it. This ability is rooted in our consciousness and free will. In contrast, animals are driven to satisfy their needs only at the level of instinct. They eat when they are hungry, store food as winter approaches, build nests when it is time to lay eggs. While on the one hand they crave only that which they need, on the other they cannot exercise freedom of choice or imagine ways of improving their lifestyle. Desire is experienced only by humans and is ultimately the capacity which is meant to draw us toward our final goal, union with God. It makes it possible for us to image and long for that which will satisfy us.

Desire is essentially an innate emptiness deep within us which craves to be filled, and can ultimately be filled only with God. But it also serves us by leading us to improve the material, intellectual and spiritual quality of our lives, thus developing our human potential. Yet so often this second, temporal aspect of desire distracts us from recognizing and responding to our root desire which is an intrinsic part of our very being and can be satisfied only in God. Rather than serving us, our temporal desires for material possessions and security can lead us on a tangent, away from the fulfillment which we really desire if we allow them to consume our attention. We never seem to learn that we will soon tire of our new clothes, lose our taste for yogurt, and look for Alka Seltzer after devouring a second dessert.

Usually it is only after years of spinning round and round and reaching out for brass rings that we realize our arm is getting tired, and we still have that restless yearning within us. Even managing to be successful in grasping the ring and tossing it skillfully into the clown's wide open mouth only gives us a passing thrill.

Coming to this realization is commonly referred to as the mid-life crisis. At this transition point some of us find that

79

all we have achieved up to now seems good, but unfulfilling. We yearn for something that will give more meaning to our lives, fulfill a potential not yet explored. Others are confronted with a devastating feeling that everything that they thought they had accomplished is worthless. Their lives have been a waste of time and they see no direction for the future. They sink into depression with no energy or confidence to look toward the future. Whichever the case, we find ourselves on a bridge over a deep chasm, familiar with that which is behind us and uncertain about what lies ahead. Should we move forward to face unknown challenges, or is it better to return to a secure, if unfulfilling, routine? Should we simply resign ourselves to being content with what we have, spiritually, materially and in our relationships?

This is a crucial decision. To turn back is to settle for a sterile security rather than to strive for a sense of fulfillment; to move ahead is to take the risk of becoming all that it is possible for us to be, and that may require radical change. Walking across the bridge may lead us into a new consciousness of our relationship with God and thus bring about a deepening of our spiritual life. Such a deepening may lead us through darkness before showing us the light of his presence. Crossing the bridge may present us with new opportunities for education or ministry. It may make us more acutely aware of others' needs and fill us with the urge to reach out to touch their lives. Whatever concrete form a mid-life transition takes, if our choices are prompted by our deepest Self and if we have the courage to trust and follow that inner voice, we will discover amazing potential and opportunities for attaining what we really desire.

Too often at transition points in our lives we are like the Samaritan woman standing at the well, our attention so intently focused on the proximate goal of getting water to slake our thirst that we fail to recognize the opportunity to ask for living water that will quench our radical thirst for union with God and eternal life. (Jn 4:1–14) Our need for an immediate solution to our problems is so intense that we forget that if we desire first the kingdom of God, "all these other things will be given you as well." (Mt 6:33) This is not to say that we should not attempt to solve our problems and drop the bucket into the well of our own resources, but when our passing needs blind us to the core desire at the center of our being, the desire for true life, they destroy us.

In one of my more philosophical dreams, which seldom occur, I am a student in a class. The teacher asks, "Who can give me a definition of value?" I excitedly raise my hand, sure that I know the answer: "What you value is a preferred object of desire. You value what you desire and desire what you value." It is true that our desires reveal much about our real values. The dream statement led me to reflect on the dichotomy between what I say I value most, and what my desires indicate that I value. My day to day choices and decisions are motivated by what I desire, whether I am ready to admit that or not, and my desires arise out of my values. Do I really value "living water," eternal life, more than water that will quench my thirst only momentarily? I may be more anxious to preserve my own comfort than to share my goods and my time with the poor, to look for fun and relaxation during my free time than to spend a few moments in prayer.

Consciousness, desire, and the freedom to choose are awesome gifts because they bring with them responsibility for our own actions. They are meant to be a means to attaining eternal life, but we can so easily use them to our own detriment and allow them to enslave us. How can that happen? It can happen only if we try to satisfy our deep sense of emptiness with such things as material goods, status, security and success. Focusing all of our attention on those passing satisfactions blinds us to the one thing necessary which will give us peace. In contrast, if we "seek first the kingdom of God," then all of our other desires fall into place in the proper order. We can satisfy them and they will not consume us. That sounds too simple to be true. We have heard that solution so many times that we no longer listen

81

to it. Yet there are parallels even on the level of everyday life which may help us understand it.

The other day I heard an insurance commercial on the radio. Firemen are shouting orders, sirens and cries of panic fill the air. A home is burning and a mother standing outside calls out desperately for someone to save her child who is still in the house. A fireman finally brings the child to her mother, saying, "Here is your daughter, but I'm not sure we can save your house." I'm sure that at that moment the mother was so overjoyed that her child was safe that she barely heard what the fireman said. Her thoughts were not on material possessions, but on the child whom she loved above all else. Her marvelous insurance coverage was probably the last thing she was thinking about.

Love made all other values fall into place, put them into proper perspective. Our love for God does the same. It does not destroy our capacity to desire and enjoy temporal goods, it simply puts them in their place so that they do not dominate our lives and consume us.

Singleness of desire channels all of our energies toward that which we most desire. It does not mean that we will no longer experience fear and dread of losing something that is important to us, but that fear will not control us. We will feel lesser desires. That is human. But we will be freed from their control over our emotions and actions, and experience the freedom of the children of God.

We see this in the lives of the saints. They were characterized by a singleness of purpose which was motivated by their tremendous love for God. But this did not extinguish their ability to enjoy created things, their desire to succeed at what they were doing, their need for human support and love; rather all of these things were included within the spotlight of their one love and enhanced by that light. Teresa of Avila enjoyed dancing at recreation periods; Francis of Assisi relished a delicacy that was brought to him by Lady Jacoba even as he lay dying. Sanctity does not destroy human desire, but builds on it.

The secret of sanctity is to desire what God desires, to unite our will with God's will. That alone brings true peace and ends the tension and conflict within us. God's will is not a force that is imposed on us from on high, but it is experienced as an impulse or attraction deep within us. What God desires, then, is not something separate from our own wishes. Deep down we really want what is for our good, and that is exactly what God wants for us. The problem is often with discerning which of our desires tend toward that good. Consequently, all too often, although we are aware of God's desire within us, we decide not to respond to it and listen rather to another desire that is screaming to be fulfilled. One of my favorite holy cards is a photograph of St. Thérèse of Lisieux as a young girl. Beneath the photograph is this sentence in her own handwriting, "Mon Dieu, je choisis tout ce que vous voulez." My God, I choose all that you will. She might have said, "My God, I desire all that you desire." Thérèse must have dreaded pain, fatigue and misunderstanding, and feared death just as we do, but she so desired God that that desire consumed her. She wanted to be united with him whom she loved, no matter what the cost.

St. John of the Cross, a sixteenth century Spanish mystic, is one who has written much about desire, expressing this very truth in poetic images. Yet he is so often viewed as the ultimate ascetic who calls Christians to crush every desire except the desire for God. His asceticism can be perceived as a negative, all-inclusive denial of human satisfaction. Reading his poetry, however, one sees that the contrary is true. John celebrates life and enjoys its beauty with the freedom of one who loves God so much that he is unencumbered by other attachments and dependencies. The reason his writing is misunderstood is that readers, fearing that they cannot understand his mystical poetry, turn too quickly to his commentaries in which he explains the verses line by line. They forget that this explanation was written in the cultural context of sixteenth century Spain with examples and directives the people of that time understood.

They found his ecstatic description of the spiritual life in his poetry too good to be true, just as we do.

John's advice is not that we crush our natural, human desires, but rather that we allow them to be transformed. His formula for that in Book One of *The Ascent of Mount Carmel* is simple: first, focus on Christ and imitate him in all things; then, out of love for him, do not desire any other satisfaction. What so many readers fail to notice is that he goes on to say that we will experience other satisfactions, and that is all right. The clue is that we must not yearn for these pleasures because that yearning might then overshadow our desire for Christ and lead us away from him. The key, then, is desire. As our love and longing for Christ grow, that desire transforms all other yearnings, just as the mother's love for her child left in the burning house transformed her desire to save her material possessions from being destroyed by fire. Of course, she would have been elated if the fire could have been controlled and her home saved, but that desire for material things was secondary to her love for her child.

Understanding the importance of this ordering of our desires is essential for spiritual growth. For example, in our approach to Christian asceticism, we too often put the cart before the horse. We set out on a Lenten regime designed to develop self-discipline and get all of our passions under control, as if will-power and determination were all that were necessary. We manage to keep our resolutions for forty days, giving up candy, attending Mass every morning, undertaking a regime worthy of the desert fathers and then wonder why we feel exhausted as if released from prison instead of renewed and filled with new life on Easter. Simply throwing cold water on all of our desires for six weeks will not destroy them, but seems rather to give them new strength so that we are soon back to our old patterns.

The value of self-denial depends on our motive. If it is undertaken as a program of self-improvement to conquer our will and make us a better person, it has little lasting effect except to bolster our pride if we are successful. If, on the other hand, it is a natural response to our desire to imitate Christ and to love him more than all else, including ourselves, then it is the love which motivates it that gives it value and transforms us.

That is why John of the Cross does not begin by telling us to deny our every desire for pleasure, as if that would lead us to union with God. He tells us to begin by nourishing our love for Jesus by reading the Gospels and learning to know him. Then our love for him will bring us to turn away from everything which is an obstacle to that love. Our desires for human pleasures become an obstacle only when they are greater than our desire for Jesus.

In his *Spiritual Canticle* John describes the bride searching for her beloved so intently that she does not "gather flowers" along the way. To pick the flowers would not only distract her from her search, but clinging to them would soon destroy their beauty and she would soon only throw them away. This parallels what we do in life. We are continually picking flowers and clutching them tightly instead of enjoying their beauty in a natural setting. Seeing something that pleases us, one more brass ring, we reach out for it and hold it fast, only to find that its attraction fades, so we discard it and look for something else. We continually wish we had something better—a television with remote control, a cordless phone, a car with air conditioning; the list goes on and on. These wishes are not wrong unless gathering these flowers distracts us from our search for our Beloved.

Sometimes our desires for temporal things, a promotion at work, a meaningful relationship, or even the restored health of a loved one, can be like handcuffs that restrict our freedom. They rivet our attention on one concern so effectively that other good things are placed in the shadows, whether it be our love for our family or our love for God. Then, for the moment, we are held captive by our own desires. That is why Jesus encourages us so frequently in the Gospels to deny ourselves, to take up our cross, to lose our life that we might save it. These actions, like our Lenten resolutions, can only be effective if they are undertaken in the light of Jesus' presence, out of love, not as ends in themselves. His message was no more negative than John's. He knew that true freedom and joy lie in not allowing ourselves to be handcuffed by our desires for temporal things. He wanted us to be free.

A poignant example of this is given in the account of the rich young man who asks Jesus what he must do to gain eternal life. He says, "There is only one thing that I really want, and that is to live forever." Jesus answers simply that he must keep the commandments. The young man is not satisfied with that answer because he thinks he already keeps the commandments. Jesus knows that this is not completely true. The first great commandment is to love the Lord your God with your whole heart, to desire him more than all else. The young man is obviously filled with other desires that take precedence in his life, so Jesus spells out more specifically what lies at the root of his problem. He tells the man, "Go, sell all that you have; get rid of all that is in the way of loving the Lord your God; get rid of the false gods in your life; free yourself of all that you are clinging to, not just possessions, but everything: status, family, friends, security, and then come, follow me." The story gives every indication that the man was leading a good life, not misusing his riches, but his desire to amass wealth was obviously in the way of his desire to follow Jesus, for at Jesus' words he went away sad. (Lk 11:22)

In our own lives it is so difficult to identify what we really desire most. Like the rich young man, we may think that we desire eternal life more than anything else. But do we? Do our choices and our use of time show that is our greatest desire? What desire gets in the way of our following Christ? That is a hard question to answer, but it is worth pondering. Our eternal life may depend on it!

One indication of where our attachments lie is found in our worries and fears. These are concerns that that which we desire and cling to will be taken from us, perhaps our loved ones, our independence, or our life itself. We might ask ourselves then what worries us, what awakens fear within us? These emotions, which often have a strength that seems disproportionate to the situation in which we find ourselves, can be a means to knowing ourselves better. They put a spotlight on our values and show us our attachments.

Desire is an integral part of being human. It is the root energy at the core of our existence. Our challenge is not to destroy desire, but to channel it so that it carries us toward the happiness for which we were created. It is desire which either fuels our love and enables us to let go of self-centeredness that we might reach out of ourselves to others and to God, or turns us in upon ourselves. It can be like a music that leads us to move in balanced rhythm, or like a lead weight that pulls us down into the morass of selfishness.

There are two levels of desire within us: the desire for ordinary things whether material, psychological, or intellectual, and the desire for All, for God himself. If our desire for God and all that he desires is primary, then all other desires can be included in and transformed by that one love. On the contrary, if desire for ordinary things takes precedence in our lives, these can become idols and destroy our relationship with God. St. Thérèse of Lisieux was able to delight in the ordinary because she first said, "I choose all." Her radical desire for God freed her to desire other things without becoming entangled in the web of conflicting desires.

At our deepest center we have only one desire, to live and to love, but we have splintered that desire into multiple wishes so that the root energy which motivates us becomes tangential and leads us away from this single desire for All. How often, as we reach out for one brass ring after another, we have said, "I feel pulled in all directions." "My energies are scattered." We know that all that we are doing is good in itself, yet we sense that something is not right. We have lost the balance and unity in our life. These multiple desires and choices must be pulled back into their proper place and ordered. If they become our primary concern, we make them idols which prevent our satisfying our greatest desire.

Restoring things to their proper perspective is more easily said than done. We fail time after time because our usual approach is to attack one desire or activity at a time following the principle of divide and conquer. This simply is not effective because it only focuses our attention on the problem, thus distancing us more and more from that which we really desire. As we restore one desire to its proper place, another one takes over. A logical, management style approach to reordering our priorities offers at best only a temporary solution. I speak from experience.

So many times in my life I have found myself over-extended, over-involved, immersed in doing many good things, so that "the one thing necessary," that which I thought I most desired, was pushed to the background. I would then resolve to cut back on activities and take more time for prayer, but because I was concentrating more on the cutting back and on my own efforts than on the prayer, the remedy was always temporary. I would soon find myself over-extended again, doing many good things, but neglecting the one Good. The real solution was to begin to be more attentive to my greatest desire, to begin to spend more time in prayer. There I found myself at the still point in the center of the cyclone, and I was able to be attentive to my desire for God and enkindle that flame. Then other priorities gradually fell into place; some activities became less important than my desire to respond to God's call. Other desires for certain kinds of ministry, professional status and success, some pleasures and satisfactions were gently transformed so that I could enjoy them while not being controlled by my attachment to them. I was being freed to follow my greatest desire.

When I was a child at Camp Fire Girls camp, one of my favorite songs was "Witchcraft." The first lines were:

If there were witchcraft, I'd make two wishes:
a winding road that beckons me to roam;
and then I'd wish for a blazing campfire
to welcome me when I'm returning home.

I must admit that the only "roam" I had heard of was Rome, and I wondered why anyone would wish to be beckoned to Rome! I had my own wishes, however, and probably substituted them in my reveries as I sat in front of the campfire. The prevalence of wishing in songs, folklore, fairy tales and myths speaks of the centrality of desire in every culture of all ages.

An example of this is evident in the rituals connected with wish-making which we learned as children: looking at the first evening star, blowing out birthday candles, and breaking wishbones. Then we heard tales of fairy godmothers or of genies who popped out of magic lamps and offered to grant three wishes. A recurring motif in these stories is that the first two wishes a person makes are self-centered and bring disaster, so the third wish is used to return things to the way they were before the wishing began. That reflects a common pattern in our lives. At first our desires are focused on what we want for ourselves. The result can be somewhat disastrous. Only as we mature do we realize that "it is in giving that we receive." Our true happiness is not found in satisfying all our passing desires; in fact attempting to do that may even destroy our happiness. It is like eating a whole jar of jelly beans. Each morsel is delicious, but the end result is a stomach ache. With maturity we learn to identify our deepest desire which leads us out of ourselves before using up our third wish.

The three wishes might be compared to three stages of life. During the first stage our choices are largely based on impulse. We are fired by our enthusiasm and newly found independence and, consequently, make some wrong decisions. Then, in our thirties and forties we become more reflective and discern that some of the choices we made in our earlier years were not the best, so we make the necessary adjustments in our priorities. With the wisdom that comes in our later years we find that we have learned from the mistakes we have made as well as from the success we have had, and we seek to use the time of our third wish to bring unity to our life. We build on the lessons of the first two stages of life.

The task of discerning our true desire and of reexamining our priorities is life-long. It is as if there were two drives within us, each urging us to walk in a different direction. In fact, that has long been the human experience. The Latin root of the word genie, that tempting little being that emerges from its magic lamp at the most unexpected times, is "genius," a tutelary deity, guide or guardian spirit allotted to a person from birth. According to Webster, one definition of genius is "either of two mutually opposed spirits, one good and the other evil, supposed to attend a person throughout his life." All of us have experienced the presence of these two genies or tendencies within us. We want to get up in the morning, but at the same time we would really rather stay in bed. Our very own genies keep popping up and tantalizing us with possibilities, whetting our appetites for good or for evil.

Even St. Paul wrote about this inward struggle, "I cannot understand my own behavior. I fail to carry out the things I want to do, and find myself doing the very things I hate." (Rom 7:15–16) Any one of us could repeat those same words. We could echo his frustration as we see ourselves time and time again failing to follow our deepest desire for good, and instead listening to the evil genie within us. It is reassuring to read Paul's words of encouragement in the next chapter of his Letter to the Romans in which he reminds us that "the law of the spirit of life in Christ Jesus has set you free from the law of sin and death." (Rom 8:2) The evil genie no longer has power over us. We are free to choose to follow the promptings of the Spirit.

When Yahweh gave Moses the first formal laws or commandments which were to govern the lives of the Israelites, these too were laws designed to bring us life and free us from the snares laid by our evil genie that tirelessly tempts us to seek self-centered satisfactions. The ten commandments are intended to prevent us from allowing an unbridled desire to destroy us. Our God cautions us in this way: "Do not desire something so much that you kill someone, or steal, or commit adultery to satisfy your craving. Do not desire your own way so much that you forget to honor your father and your mother. Do not desire a material thing so much that you covet your neighbor's goods. Be careful not to desire anything so intensely that you make it a false god. Instead, remember to desire the Lord your God, and love him above all things."

Observing these commandments will preserve peace and happiness both within ourselves and throughout the world. Balancing our own desires will affect our relationships with everyone, not only with those whom we encounter, but with every person throughout the world, because in unseen ways we are united with all people. Allowing ourselves to get caught up in the whirlwind of consumerism which continually fuels our desires for material goods not only brings us pain, but contributes to the oppression of millions of people in the third world.

As early as the sixth century before Christ, Buddha searched for a way to achieve true peace and put an end to suffering. He too focused on desire or attachment. In his First Sermon he presents a straightforward and deceptively simple way to free ourselves from suffering and thus find peace. His solution is this: because suffering is caused by attachment to things and by our desire for these things, the way to free ourselves from suffering is to eliminate attachment and desire for things.

To a point there is great similarity between Buddha's solution and Christ's teaching. Both tell us that we must deny ourselves and be detached from temporal things in order to find happiness. But while according to Buddha's method one begins with detachment in order to be freed from suffering, in Christ's teaching one begins with love for God which leads us to detachment from other desires and brings true happiness. Our reason for denying the fulfillment of some desires must always be love of God, or the denial will simply leave us with a great void. Jesus, like Buddha, urges us to empty ourselves, to let go of attachment to earthly desires, but there the similarity ends. Buddha promises that we will be free from suffering, while Jesus promises that we will be filled with the peace and joy of his presence. He knows that our tendency to fill ourselves with earthly delights can cause us to forget our greatest desire which is union with God, and thus can lead us to great unhappiness.

Unfortunately, it is all too easy to be enticed by the good things of this world and to lose our balance. If Jesus were to tell us a parable today, it might be something like this:

> There was once a little girl who loved to ride merry-go-rounds and reach out to catch the brass rings. She would clutch the brass pole tightly as her brightly colored horse moved up and down to the music. Then each time she came close to the brass ring she would hold her breath in excitement, grab the ring and toss it toward the smiling mouth of the clown face. She concentrated so hard on hooking her finger through the ring that sometimes she didn't even hear the music or notice the people around her. The clown face seemed to laugh at her if she didn't have a ring to throw at it as she flew by. One day in her determination to grab the ring she let go of the pole and reached out with both hands just to be sure. But the little girl lost her balance and fell to the ground. A sharp pain shot through her arm. As she lay there the merry-go-round kept turning, the music kept playing, her horse went on without her, and the clown face was still laughing.

8

CAVES AND NICHES

Rain penetrating the forest, branches breaking from trees, water tumbling over rocks in the creek . . . sounds that can only be heard in silence break the very silence that embraces them. Nature fills the spaces of solitude.

Enveloped in the stillness of my hermitage, listening to the murmuring fire in the wood stove, I watch the floating waves of smoke from the chimney invade the cool freshness of the forest air. The green of the tall, proud redwood trees and the glistening, wet leaves of the madrones contrast sharply with the misty air, providing a backdrop for the gentle sound of the rain and the singing of the windchimes. The soft beauty of the moment adds to my sense of being in a sacred space of solitude and deepens my awareness of being immersed in the presence of God.

In a pensive mood I begin to wonder at the events in my life which have led me to this solitary time and space, and gradually begin a dialogue with an inner voice.

"Why am I here? How has it happened that I should be living in solitude deep in the silence of the forest?"

"Why do you ask?"

"I guess it is my amazement that prompts the question. Sometimes I think I know the answer, and at other moments I am left with a sense of wonder."

"The why and the how do not matter. Those are feeble attempts to know with the mind that which is beyond human reason. A neatly packaged answer to why you are here only distracts you from a deeper truth. A response to how it has happened only leads you to a series of events that have preceded this moment. Neither is relevant."

"What is the question that I should ask?"

"There is only one that matters: Where?"

"Where am I?"

"You are immersed in the silent Word of God. That is all it is important to know, the only answer that matters. All that surrounds you is there to lead you deeper into an awareness of that presence. The externals of your life make no difference if you can remember where you are . . . in God."

Reflecting on these thoughts, I realize that to live in solitude is to live in mystery. It involves both space and time, but the true solitude is a space at my deepest center where I meet my God. Whether in the midst of the soft forest rain, the crisp summer sunshine of the valley, or the hubbub of the city, no explanation is needed of how or why I am there, only a realization of where I am, immersed in God and filled with God. I must simply be, be who I am, be who God created me to be without seeking to know the answers. The focus is on being in the presence of God, rather than on knowing and doing.

This is what happens in solitude as one is stripped of the purposefulness that seems to come with action, and gifted with the emptiness of being. It is only in accepting emptiness that one can be filled; only in being filled with an awareness of God's intimate presence that one can allow that presence to overflow into others' lives.

While few are called to live in a hermitage, everyone experiences times and places of external solitude, pleasant or unpleasant, chosen or imposed. Everyone also enters at times into an interior space of aloneness and apparent emptiness, sometimes of loneliness, sometimes of peace. This is an integral part of the ebb and flow of human life: activity followed by quiet, being with others and then alone, sharing our most intimate thoughts or standing in the isolation of misunderstanding. Both exterior and interior solitude weave in and out of everyone's life, but it is our attitude toward our inner space that colors our vision of external aloneness. It is this attitude which causes us to seek or fear, to accept or shun these times of being alone.

Many walk away from the solitary moment or space, seeing only its emptiness, or hasten to camouflage it with sound and activity. Thus they destroy its power to open the heart to wisdom, because they fail to recognize the potential of solitude to provide a still space where one can hear an inner voice that speaks of truth. Paradoxically, others yearn for times of quiet aloneness in the midst of their busy lives, perceiving the treasure within themselves and wanting to explore its riches. Solitary times and spaces remove the static from our lives and allow us to hear the voice from our deepest Self, the voice of our God who often speaks to us without words in the midst of silence.

We all remember interior moments of solitude that cannot be shared, that must be savored or endured alone. Caught up in the soaring notes of a symphony, the vibrant hues of a silent sunset, the pounding rhythm of the surf, or struggling to accept the diminishment of illness, the separation from a loved one, an unjust accusation, each one of us stands alone. No one can share the exquisite joy or the penetrating pain that we feel. The experience of solitude may be one of ecstasy or sadness, tedium or excitement, or simply peaceful stillness, but it always has the quality of being unique to the person and impossible to describe.

We yearn for solitary times and places that are of our own choosing, and fear those which are thrust upon us. Perhaps that is the difference between being alone and being lonely. The first is a state of being, neither good nor bad in itself; the latter is a negative reaction to that state. It would follow, then, that if we could learn to treasure all moments of solitude, we would never be lonely.

I was talking with someone recently who spoke of an experience she and her husband had of being snowed in while they were staying in a mountain cabin. When they heard that a storm was predicted, they were actually looking forward to the time they would have together in front of a blazing fireplace. Yet, when it happened, they became restless and uneasy and could not relax and enjoy the experience. They realized the difference lay in their loss of freedom. They were no longer able to choose to stay in the cabin; they were held captive.

The key to learning to value all moments of solitude is in our attitude, acceptance and openness to the experience. But first, we have to recognize the possibilities of the moment. It seems almost impossible to look positively even at times of darkness and suffering, but seeing their potential does not necessarily imply enjoying them. Nevertheless, they too hold a gift we all too readily refuse.

Times and spaces of solitude, both interior and exterior, present themselves to us under various guises. If we long for an idealized place of quiet where we can escape from the hectic pace of life even for a little while, we are apt to miss the opportunities that are already available within our daily lives. Just as God called the prophets of old to sacred spaces where they would be quiet enough to hear his voice, just as he called the early hermits to the desert or mountain wilderness so that they might be attentive to him, so also he calls us to wilderness places. In our modern world he fashions new sacred, solitary spaces where we can be alone and free from the distractions that drown out his words. These may be so much a part of our lives that we overlook them, seeking instead a special place apart. The space to which God calls us, however, is always in our deepest center, whether in an atmosphere of external solitude or in the midst of activity.

We must all learn to identify our own caves and niches where we can be alone with our God. Ironically, we are sometimes most alone and find our interior sacred space when we are surrounded by people, anonymous in a crowd. The deserts of everyday life are as commonplace as driving alone in freeway traffic, standing in a long line at a supermarket checkout, walking on a crowded city street. At times like this I feel almost invisible.

I am especially aware of this anonymity of modern society when I contrast it with the years that I lived in a small town in Spain where there were no supermarkets or busy streets. I bought fresh fruits and vegetables at open air stalls from women who brought their own produce in from the fields. Then I walked to a poultry store, a bread shop, another small store where I bought milk, a bodega where I filled my own bottle with wine from a keg. I had to allow a couple of hours for these purchases because each one meant an encounter with a person and a friendly conversation. I recently returned there after an absence of ten years, and doing my shopping was like a reunion with friends. I was amazed that the people remembered me. Here I can go into a supermarket week after week and never be recognized because there is no personal encounter there. It is one of the deserts of modern times.

The anonymity of contemporary society can be a wilderness that provides the environment conducive to an inner encounter with God. Times and spaces when one is lost in a crowd can be savored as gifts of silence. In our age a wilderness experience is often not physical, but psychological or spiritual. It can, nonetheless, be an opportunity for solitude if only we recognize it. Becoming aware of the caves and niches of our everyday lives is a challenge because we tend to fill them with the noise of our thoughts and plans, with conversation or with a novel, so that the quiet they offer is shattered. Because exterior solitude is difficult to achieve, we fail to cultivate the interior solitude which is always available.

In short, our reaction to interior or exterior solitary moments in our lives is always an outgrowth of our relationship to the solitude within us. If we are in touch with our center and comfortable with our true Self, we will value opportunities that allow us to spend time in that inner sacred space, for in the end all solitude is experienced deep within the person. While some times of solitude may be set in a milieu of external aloneness which either forces us or invites us to enter into that inner space, the awareness of being alone before God is the true existential solitude that can only be known at our own deepest center.

In scripture there are many instances in which a space of external isolation provides the milieu for an encounter with God. In Genesis we read of the time that Jacob was sent to Paddan-aram to choose a wife. At the end of the first day's journey he found a solitary place to spend the night, chose a stone for a pillow, and lay down on the ground.

> He had a dream: a ladder was there, standing on the ground with its top reaching to heaven; and there were angels of God going up it and coming down. And Yahweh was there, standing over him, saying, "I am Yahweh, the God of Abraham your father, and the God of Isaac. I will give to you and your descendants the land on which you are lying...." Then Jacob awoke from his sleep and said, "Truly Yahweh is in this place and I never knew it." (Gen 28:10–17)

This account is rich in symbolism, as is the case with dreams. The ladder is a significant image of the two-way communication which we must expect in any experience of God. Jacob's receptivity, demonstrated by his obedience in allowing himself to be sent into the wilderness, and his silence as he lay down to sleep paved the way for the words of Yahweh to be heard in his dream. An encounter with God involves some readiness on our part. Aside from the promise which Yahweh made to Jacob that night, perhaps the most meaningful sentence of the passage is "Truly Yahweh is in this place and I never knew it." This was a moment of enlightenment and conversion for Jacob. He was startled by a message that was spoken from within his unconscious, but he did not hesitate to accept its truth. Yahweh was not only in the place where Jacob had chosen to spend the night, he was in the sacred space within Jacob.

Jacob had another awesome experience later when he again spent the night alone in the wilderness. He found himself wrestling with an unknown adversary who refused to tell him his name. But in the morning "Jacob named the place Peniel, 'Because I have seen God face to face,' he said, 'and I have survived.' " (Gen 32:31) That encounter left Jacob wounded and limping, but strengthened for his meeting with his brother Esau whom he had cheated out of his inheritance many years before. Some solitary spaces into which we are called are places of struggle and pain, but if we wrestle with our fears and confront our weakness, we too can emerge as one who has been touched and transformed by God.

Sometimes our interior space seems like the lions' den into which poor Daniel was thrown. Daniel had earned the king's friendship because of his wisdom in being able to interpret a dream, and had been given authority over a large part of the kingdom. This, of course, made others jealous, so they plotted against him. Noticing that Daniel prayed to his God three times a day, they convinced the king that he should make a regulation that whoever prayed to anyone other than to the king himself within the next thirty days should be thrown into the lions' den. Then they watched Daniel who, as they had expected, continued to pray to his God. When they reported this to the king, he was saddened because Daniel was his friend, but he had no recourse but to do as he had said. He said to Daniel, "Your God himself, whom you have served so faithfully, will have to save you." At dawn the king hurried to the lions' den and found that Daniel's God had indeed protected him. (Dan 6)

Our own situation can be similar to Daniel's. Although

we try to be faithful to prayer, fulfill our duties, respond to others' needs and, in general, lead a good life, we can suddenly find ourselves in the midst of a dark pit filled with the lions of depression, guilt, anger and tension. We feel overwhelmed and see no way of escape. It seems that like Daniel, the more we try to be open and responsive to God, the more apt we are to be called to confront these terrifying aspects of ourselves. At such a time all we can do is what Daniel must have done. After an initial moment of terror and helplessness, he must have cried out to Yahweh to deliver him. He certainly knew that there was nothing he could do to save himself. Yahweh heard his prayer and protected him. Daniel emerged not only unharmed, but with his faith and trust in God strengthened. The time he spent in the darkness facing the lions left its mark on him, just as Jacob's struggle with the angel left him changed.

So it is with us. The time spent alone in the darkness surrounded by our own deepest demons is also terrifying, but if we can hold on to our faith and confidence in our God who is there with us, and remember that he will not test us beyond our strength, we will experience his presence in the midst of our desperation and emerge strengthened and joyful, having passed through an ordeal. In the midst of such periods of uncertainty and suffering it is impossible to pray as we used to pray. We can only cry out for help. Although at such times we may think we cannot pray, it is usually only that the form of our prayer has changed. Admission of our own powerlessness and a plea for strength and wisdom is enough. We need to hear the words Moses spoke to the Israelites as they were fleeing from the Egyptians: "Yahweh will do the fighting for you: you have only to keep still." (Ex 14:14)

Fortunately, encounters with God in our own solitary space are usually not so frightening and do not always involve struggle. Many times of solitude and quiet prayer are very ordinary, almost tedious. Nothing seems to happen. Then too there are moments of peace and joy that far outnumber the moments of pain. We are sometimes led to a place apart so that we may catch a glimpse of eternity as did Peter, James and John on Mount Tabor. Our vision, unlike theirs, will probably be only interior, but a place of quiet, away from our everyday responsibilities and distractions, can support our entry into our inner space where we are open to the voice of God. Over the years I have found various special places to which I could withdraw for a few days from time to time in order to reflect, pray, and simply be quiet. There was a monastery in the high desert near Los Angeles, the sanctuary of Montserrat near Barcelona, a cloistered twelfth century convent in Girona, and the Camaldolese hermitage on the Pacific coast. All of these provided an atmosphere of solitude, away from my usual activities, but the environment was only a catalyst for my getting in touch with the solitary space within me.

It is not always necessary or possible, however, to find the time to go away to a place conducive to solitude. We must find the caves and niches of our daily lives where we can often spend some time alone within ourselves, and not be dependent on physical solitude which is not always available.

When I reflect on the moment when the angel Gabriel spoke to Mary, telling her she was blessed among women and about to become the mother of God, I picture the familiar paintings of the scene showing Mary kneeling quietly at prayer. She may indeed have been immersed in contemplation when she received that amazing message, but I think it is just as likely that she was drawing water from the well or doing dishes. Mary must have lived in a constant state of attentiveness to God regardless of what she was doing, having learned to treasure all opportunities to descend to the private niche she had carved in her heart for solitary times of communion with her God. She had become a sacred space long before Gabriel announced to her that the Spirit of the Most High was hovering over her and the Word was taking flesh within her. It was possible for that Word to take on our humanity in her and come forth from her to dwell in each one of us because the Word of God had already found a home in her heart. We too are challenged to create that sacred space within us so that Jesus may be incarnated in our lives and come forth from us in our daily actions.

In the midst of our hectic lives this may seem almost impossible. How can we find even a few moments during the day to quiet our thoughts and center them on God? There are family responsibilities, meetings to attend and telephone calls to make, and all of this after we have taught third grade or worked in an office all day. But somehow we find time to do what is important to us. Times of interior solitude can be found if only we know how to look. They may be discovered while we are swimming laps in a pool, taking a walk on our lunch hour, or driving home from work. A mother of a family once told me that she would sometimes stop the car on a quiet street on the way home from shopping and spend a few minutes in prayer. Any place in which we are insulated from the usual daily pressures can serve as a personal, private cave. Creative thinking can show us how to fashion secluded niches in our day.

It may help to consider what makes a space or time sacred and sets it apart. All space is potentially sacred for it can be a meeting place between the divine and human. A sacred space is a point of connection between heaven and earth where God manifests himself and human consciousness opens itself to receive the revelation. As with Jacob's ladder, there is a double movement, an ascending attitude of attentiveness on our part, and an outpouring of divine presence into our hearts. The sacredness of any place is ignited by the touch of God as was the burning bush. But God does not force his entry into the space. He awaits our readiness. A sacred space is one that is open and yearning to receive the manifestation of God, to absorb his Word and to enfold it that it may dwell there. Each one of us is created to be a sacred space, a point in time where God touches humanity and communicates himself.

Just as a sound is not heard in the wilderness unless there are ears to hear it, so also a space is only made sacred when a human person catches the whisper of the gentle breeze of God's presence and looks up in awe. The place in which I stand is sacred not only because God is revealing himself there, but because I am there to receive that revelation, not only because he speaks his Word, but because that Word resonates within me. The Spirit of God descends to that space and envelops both the divine and the created, unifying them in one breath of life.

God's encounter with humanity took on a new dimension at the incarnation. He no longer needs to speak to us in fire, earthquakes, pillars of cloud, or even gentle breezes. He dwells within each one of us: "If anyone loves me he will keep my word and my Father will love him, and we shall come to him and make our home with him." (Jn 14:23) Each one of us is called to be a sacred space!

The presence of the divinity within us has the power to transform any place where we stand into a sacred place, the kitchen, the office, the swimming pool, the supermarket, if only we are attentive to that presence. Then, too, we will become transparent, and as others become aware of the God within us they also will become attentive to his presence. Our awareness of God who makes his home in us can serve as a lightning rod to attract the Word of God that he may be incarnated in our lives. Whether like Jacob we are asleep in our wilderness, like Elijah we are hiding in our cave, or like Daniel we are beset by the beasts of our own shadows, we can learn to recognize spaces of solitude in our lives and allow them to shape us.

Jesus taught us to seek out our own interior sacred space in his conversation with the Samaritan woman at the well. His offer to give her living water if she would only ask and his knowledge that she had had five husbands made her realize that he was no ordinary man. She said he must be a prophet, and took the opportunity to bring up a controversial issue hoping he would solve it: "Our fathers worshiped on this mountain, while you say that Jerusalem is the place where one ought to worship." Jesus' response must have surprised her:

> Believe me, woman, the hour is coming
> when you will worship the Father
> neither on this mountain nor in Jerusalem. . . .
> But the hour will come—in fact it is here already—
> when true worshipers will worship the Father
> in spirit and in truth:
> that is the kind of worshiper the Father wants. (Jn 4:20–23)

Jesus was calling her, and each of us, to draw living water from our own inner well, to dare to descend into our own hearts, for the source of true life lies within us. We must no longer limit our worship of God to mountains, temples, or Sunday Mass. It can seem so much safer to confine our prayer to places of ritual where limits are well defined. It is reassuring to feel we have fulfilled our obligation to worship and are now free to go about our normal activities with a clear conscience. But Jesus removed the limitations of space and time and told us we must pray to the Father in spirit and in truth. His gift of himself in the Eucharist speaks of the importance of communal celebrations and prayer, but this is not enough. He taught his disciples to pray in the solitude of their hearts:

> But when you pray, go to your private room and, when you have shut the door, pray to your Father who is in that secret place, and your Father who sees all that is done in secret will reward you. (Mt 6:6)

All prayer, both communal and private, is essentially solitary. The outward signs of the sacraments and the external forms of the liturgy, from the soaring notes of the organ, the fragrance of the incense and the words on our lips, to the ritual genuflections, are only supports for our human needs and are meant to lead us to look within our hearts and there to meet our God. Even prayers spoken in unison with others must all spring from our inner space where we worship in spirit and in truth. But, given the need we have of physical forms and environments, given the support we experience from these externals, it is clear that paying attention to them might assist us in entering into our "secret place."

I find it helpful to create a special "prayer space" in my hermitage for times of quiet prayer. Simply going to my space and sitting down on the floor cushion in front of the crucifix on the wall serves to quiet my thoughts and center my attention on the presence of God. It is a sacred place reserved for special times of encounter with the silent Word who dwells deep within me. Other externals can add to the environment of my special place: a candle, a flower, a rock, simple things that give it a character all its own. It is my "private room" where I pray to my Father "who is in that secret place."

Another external which can add to the quality of prayer time is the position one takes at prayer. I prefer sitting in a semi-lotus posture on my prayer cushion. That helps to center me and sends a message to my brain that this is a time set apart. Others may find kneeling or sitting in a chair the most helpful position. The important aspect of body posture during prayer is that the body be comfortable enough to be forgotten yet not too relaxed, at ease and yet at attention.

Centering techniques of Eastern religions have become well known in the West in recent years. Repeating a single word or phrase, a mantra, or noticing our breathing can help to draw our attention into our inner space and free us from thoughts which are barriers to a silent encounter with God. Meditative music or a repetitive chant such as those from Taizé can also serve as quieting techniques and help to free us from distractions.

So often people tell me that they have tried all these things; they sit in their prayer space and nothing happens. I then ask what they expect to happen and they are not sure. They are searching for a feeling of prayer that they cannot really describe, but it would reassure them that they are praying and not just wasting time. We are so used to thinking of prayer in terms of words that if there are no words, we wonder if we are not praying. We have forgotten about quiet attentive listening. Feelings and words are sometimes a part of prayer, but the essence of prayer is an awareness of God, a state of being which does not necessarily imply a pious feeling. It can be a silent, wordless sense of being in God's presence.

Beginning this kind of prayer requires a letting go of preconceived expectations about what happens in prayer. It is a venture into the unknown. As I write this it is raining again. It occurs to me as I watch the rain that it too is venturing into the unknown as it falls to earth not knowing what it will be like to feel the trees and then to soak into the ground. The raindrops slide tentatively down the branches to a soft encounter with the dry earth that is yearning to receive their gift of self. It is only by letting go of the security of their cloud and falling freely into the unknown that the raindrops can meet the moment of their transformation, becoming one with the earth. Then they will spring forth in new life. Our prayer, too, involves a letting go, a falling into the unknown space of our own heart, a meeting with our God who will absorb us into himself and transform us that we might bring forth new life.

To pray is to risk transformation. We do not know what that may involve, or how we may be changed. Real prayer requires not only a deep faith, but a firm trust. It is a descent into the unknown and we know not what awaits us. And yet, we do know: our loving God awaits us! The darkness, emptiness and void that surround us as we begin become light and fullness of joy as we meet him. The challenge is to take the leap of faith and leave the security of filling our prayers with familiar words which prevent us from hearing the Word spoken in the silence of the night.

An encounter with God is sometimes a wordless moment in a timeless, sacred space. The words come only afterward as we try to name our experience or reflect on it and engrave it on our memory. The welcoming embrace of God is always silent and word-shattering.

Yet there is a danger in describing prayer in these terms. The danger is of setting up new expectations in the mind of the person who begins to enter into contemplative prayer. Quiet prayer is not all ecstasy. In fact, it can be dry, restless and filled with distractions. St. Teresa of Avila found it so difficult that she once commented that she almost had to tie herself to her chair to remain at prayer. There will be many times when we share her feelings. There may also be times when we share her experience of exquisite joy and peace. With any type of prayer, whether shared or private, the feelings we have are not the best indication of the value of our prayer. But how often we judge our prayer by how we feel, or how many distractions we have. We tend to pray with the hope that we will notice some tangible results no matter how subtle they may be. The reward or the stamp of assurance that we have prayed well is important to us. The fact is that we have no way of knowing how well we have prayed, and it really does not make any difference. What matters is that we have prayed, that we have been available to God by our attentive presence in that time and space. To do this, especially when we do not receive any tangible reward for our efforts, or even any reassurance that God is there, calls for an act of pure faith. That is prayer.

If we are going to descend to our interior cave, there to be with our God, we must learn the language of silence. We need to be content with silence and rest there in an attitude of attentive listening. But this is not to say that our inner space must always be silent, that our prayer should always be wordless. We have need of words also. There will be times when we are moved to utter simple phrases of adoration in loving praise of our God, when the events of our lives will lead us to repeated, joyful words of thanksgiving. At other times, torn with worry and concern, we will find only desperate words of petition. Recognition of how we have failed to respond to God's love will sometimes bring us to a heartfelt plea for forgiveness. Often we will simply speak of our love.

God leads us to pray in many different ways at different times. He teaches us to communicate with him and to listen to him in unique ways that are ours alone. Although spiritual writers describe the various stages of prayer in ascending order, with the silent prayer of union at the top of the list, none of them implies that as we progress to higher forms of prayer, we never return to other forms. As we learn to play the piano, we begin with single notes and progress to chords, but once we have mastered the chords we do not, therefore, neglect the single melody notes. Once we have learned to play a polka, we do not avoid the waltz. Our prayer is an intricate interplay of lights and shadows, words and silence, mountain and desert. But just as space lends balance and beauty to the shapes and colors in art and architecture, so also in our prayer there must be spaces of silence to create a balance. Solitude in whatever form, whether external or deep within the cave of our heart, is the milieu which supports those silent spaces.

Identifying the caves and niches in our days and spending time there, a few moments, a few hours or a few days, makes us receptive to the Word of God and in tune with his presence in the midst of our daily activities. Then the whole world is seen as a sacred space, transparent with the Divine Presence.

9
SHAMROCKS

Gentle sunlight touched the green hills as we drove through the Irish countryside to the lilting sounds of the tin whistle. It was a pleasant change from the misty rain that had followed us during most of our trip. Looking through the window of the bus, I was caught up in the contrasts of the land, the softly contoured hills divided by stark stone fences, thatched roofed cottages resting beside modern highways, peaceful country scenes invaded by the harsh surf of the angry sea. They spoke to me of the divisions among the people themselves, centuries-old conflict in the name of religion with roots so deep that they are forgotten in the present day prejudice. The people too intrigued me. They are a solid people formed by the contrasts of their land, with an air of stoic acceptance coupled with cheerfulness. Ireland is a country of obvious poverty and hidden wealth, the richness of a people with memories.

But in spite of my quiet reveries, I was a typical tourist who wanted to kiss the Blarney Stone, and I was determined to find a shamrock. How could I visit Ireland and not pick a shamrock? Undaunted by being told that they were out of season, I kept looking and I was rewarded when our guide discovered a small clump of sturdy shamrocks that had survived the transition from spring to summer. I was a bit disappointed at how tiny they were, looking like any nondescript patch of clover, but at least I had a shamrock!

It is remarkable how symbols have emerged and persisted through centuries of tradition to speak without words of the values and heritage of nations. The eagle, the rising sun, the fleur-de-lis each bring to mind a nation of people whose lives reflect the meaning of the symbol, but the shamrock leads us to a reality deep within the Irish heritage that has had a profound impact on the cultural values of the people. Legend tells us that the significance of the shamrock in Ireland has its origins in being a visual aid for St. Patrick when he explained the doctrine of the Trinity. That seems a rather simple fact to have caused it to become a national emblem which continues to decorate St. Patrick's Day cards and decorations every March. It could not have endured if it had not taken root in the hearts of the people as a sign of their deep faith in God.

Even today the tiny, green shamrock can serve as a focus for reflection on the mystery of our triune God, three persons sharing one nature, and also, as an extension of that truth, of our human community, a multitude of persons sharing in the one divine life. Looking at the small green leaves we can recall Jesus' words, "I am the vine, you are the branches." (Jn 15:5) I am the stem, you are the leaves.

Yet perhaps we have heard the explanation of the two mysteries that there are three persons in one God and that we form one mystical body in Christ so many times that these truths no longer amaze us and fill us with wonder. They are so vast that we are unable to grasp them, so we simply accept them intellectually as articles of faith and go on about our lives. We rationalize that since they are mysteries we can never understand, we can place them in the archives of our memory to be pulled out and dusted off from time to time, and not expect them to have much influence on our day to day actions. I don't think St. Patrick would agree, nor would St. John the Evangelist, St. Paul or Jesus himself. Maybe we should look at shamrocks, or clover, a little more intently and allow their symbolism to touch us at the point where words can no longer express meaning. That exercise can open us to hear and experience anew the realities of Trinity and community.

Our belief in the interactive love among the Father, Son and Spirit can be grounded and given new life when we notice Jesus' frequent reference to his Father as one whom he loves and who loves him. "As the Father has loved me, so have I loved you." (Jn 15:9) But he does not leave the statement at the level of the Godhead. He draws us into the relationship: " ... you will understand that I am in my Father and you in me and I in you ... anybody who loves me will be loved by my Father, and I shall love him and show myself to him." (Jn 14:20–21) Then he goes one step further and draws a circle around all who believe in him, creating a community which is bonded together by the very unity of the Father and the Son in the Spirit:

> May they all be one.
> Father, may they be one in us,
> as you are in me and I am in you,
> so that the world may believe it was you who sent me.
> I have given them the glory you gave to me,
> that they may be one as we are one.
> With me in them and you in me,
> may they be so completely one
> that the world will realize that it was you who sent me
> and that I have loved them as much as you love me. (Jn
>   17:21–23)

As we read and reread those words, the mystery of the Trinity becomes a little less distant. It is firmly inserted into our lives. The love among the persons of the triune God not only touches our individual relationship with God, but it gives meaning to who we are and to our everyday interactions with those who come into our lives. We actually are one with God and with each other. The triple leaves of the shamrock then remind us not only of the three persons in God, but of the energies of their love which permeate us and make it possible for us to love our God, ourselves, and others with the love of the Spirit who dwells within us.

But what does it mean to be one with each other as Jesus is one with his Father? These realities still lie so far beyond the grasp of our understanding that we are tempted to set them aside again and turn to more down-to-earth directives of the Gospel such as "Love your neighbor as your-self." (Mk 2:31) Reflection on that straightforward imperative brings to mind a friend who called me this morning just to say hello, the mailman who took the trouble to pay the postage-due on my letter, the young girl who so cheerfully carried my groceries to the car for me. These are my neighbors. It is easy to love them. But as much as I love myself? I'm not sure that is possible. Then I remember the woman at the insurance office who was so rude to me yesterday, the man who took the parking place I was waiting for, terrorists who kill innocent people. Do I love them? At this point I am tempted to return to a meditation on the Trinity, or to go for a walk and pick some clover.

How can we ever come to the point of really loving everyone else as much as we love ourselves? How can we ever develop an awareness of our participation in the love of the Trinity? How can we ever realize that we all share in one divine life? By our own efforts we cannot. But nothing is impossible to God. Do we really believe even that? Perhaps a story will help.

A tall young man was striding purposefully along the hot, dusty road, oblivious of his companions, unaware of the parched countryside. Immersed in the mosaic of his own thoughts, he smiled with satisfaction as his mind leapt among the brightly colored memories of his past achievements. He felt an energy that was fired by the conviction that he was performing a necessary work, protecting the law and the tradition of his people. After all, many praised him for his relentless zeal in searching out those who were threatening to divide the people by their absurd belief in the resurrection of a dead man, a rabble-rouser who claimed to be the messiah. The praise made his unpleasant task seem worthwhile. It was easy to imagine himself like the prophets of old, out to destroy those who worshiped false gods.

His work was proceeding slowly, but it was better that way, better to be thorough and still give people a chance to see the light. There were times when he was discouraged at the magnitude of his task. These fanatics were amazingly steadfast in their belief in Jesus. But today, quickening his stride as he approached Damascus, he was filled with confidence. Words of the twenty-eighth psalm came to his lips, "Repay them for their actions, Yahweh, for the evil they commit, for their handiwork repay them, let them have what they deserve."

He had to admit to himself that a few months ago he could not have imagined that he would ever be involved in the death of fellow Jews. The realization left him a little uneasy at times, but then he remembered his God. This was his work. He depended on him to guide his steps. "Yahweh, teach me your way, lead me in the path of integrity." (Ps 27) Suddenly a blaze of light filled the countryside. Terrified, he fell to the ground as if pushed by an invisible force! He lay there as if paralyzed for what seemed like an endless moment, his thoughts whirling in a confused tangle. Then struggling to get up, he opened his eyes to darkness. He could not see! From somewhere deep within him came words that seemed to resound all around him,

"Saul, Saul, why are you persecuting me?"
"Who are you, Lord?"
"I am Jesus, and you are persecuting me." (Acts 9:4–6)

He knew the voice, but it couldn't be. The man was dead! Who was speaking? What did he mean? Saul's terror was intensified by his blindness. As if in a trance, he helplessly submitted to his companions' assistance and allowed them to lead him into the city. "I am Jesus, and you are persecuting me." Jesus was dead. Wasn't he?

In the obscurity of his blindness Saul began the journey to an inner vision of a profound reality. Stripped of his self-sufficiency he was forced to depend on others, to enter into a new form of relationship with them. He was no longer the proud, capable young man, so sure of himself. He was bewildered and frightened. What was he to do? He began to

117

wonder about the Christians. Was Jesus living in these people whom he was persecuting?

Saul was an intelligent, well-educated Jew, but it was not his brilliant reasoning which brought him to grasp the truth that Jesus is the eternal expression of the living God. It was an overwhelming experience which transformed Saul the Pharisee into Paul the Christian, an experience of God first through inner revelation and then through the community of believers. Later, writing to the Philippians he reflected on the tremendous upheaval in his life that had resulted from his experience with Jesus that had begun so abruptly on the road to Damascus.

> As for the law, I was a Pharisee; as for working for religion, I was a persecutor of the Church; as far as the law can make you perfect, I was faultless. But because of Christ, I have come to consider all these advantages that I had as disadvantages. Not only that, but I believe nothing can happen that will outweigh the supreme advantage of knowing Christ Jesus my Lord. For him I have accepted the loss of everything, and look on everything as so much rubbish if only I can have Christ and be given a place in him. (Phil 3:6–9)

Saul's conversion was radical. Ours too must be all consuming, fired by our continual experience of Jesus. Our faith is deepened and actualized both by the voice of the Spirit within us and by his reaching us through others. There is no separation between those two realities.

The problem is that we suffer from a kind of double vision that divides spiritual realities in two. We talk of the dynamic, interactive love which flows between the Father and the Son in the Spirit, and of the love of our Father who sent his only Son to redeem us as if they were separate actions. We talk of our love of God and our love of neighbor as if they were two distinct expressions of love. We talk of prayer and activity as opposite ways of loving, one vertical and one horizontal. We will never approach an awareness of our participation in the life of the triune God and of our sharing in this life and love with all other women and men until, like St. Paul, we are so united with the Word of God within us that our vision becomes focused on that Word. Then all reality and all of our actions will be seen enclosed in the circle of one light. That light of God has an intense power that strips away our artificiality, melts our resistance, and liberates our true Self.

But how can we even begin to experience God as Paul did? Is that total transformation within the grasp of ordinary Christians? Perhaps a more difficult question to ask is if we have the courage to risk it. Change is frightening. Paul was terrified but, as he later attested, what he was given in Christ made all that he had had in his former way of life, the power, adulation, security and respect, seem like rubbish. It could not be compared with the profound peace and joy he now knew.

We will probably not be given a sudden revelation of the Trinity, but rather God will show us glimpses of his love through concrete examples just as Patrick tried to express the mystery of the triune God by holding a tiny shamrock before his listeners. Our love for God is a sharing in the love which is God. Our love for our neighbor is a participation in that same love. And what can be even more difficult to believe is that our love for ourselves is also a participation in God's love for us. What all of this means is that we gradually come to grasp the inner love of the Trinity by experiencing that same love within ourselves. Love is never static. It reaches out. It transforms. We cannot love God without loving our neighbor, and basic to this potential to love is a strong love of ourselves.

One of the pivotal reasons that we have difficulty relating to God or to each other sometimes is that we do not really like, much less love, ourselves. We might be the last to realize and admit this, but our actions belie our basic insecurity. Our perception of others is clouded by our own shortcomings and unwittingly we project them onto others.

Even our concept of God is influenced by our limitations. If we cannot forgive ourselves, we doubt that God can forgive us either. When someone makes us angry, when we are irritated by a friend, or when we are impatient with a family member who takes us for granted, it is probably because we are not at peace within ourselves. Our sense of community and oneness with those with whom we come in contact or with people all over the world depends on our self-acceptance and our sense of unity within ourselves.

This was impressed upon me a few years ago when I was trying to identify the basic elements necessary in forming a religious community. I gathered my thoughts, as I often do, in the form of a written dialogue with my inner guide whom I introduced in a previous chapter. The ideas that came to me surprised me because I had never considered the primary importance of the individual's attitude toward himself or herself in forming community, nor the connection between the Trinity and community. I include this dialogue here not as a complete description of important aspects of community, but because it presents some thoughts about community that are often not considered. What is said about community applies to any kind of human relationship, or, to state it another way, to our love of neighbor in general.

"Kevin, what do you think of as basic elements necessary to form community. Just what is community?"

"Carole, the important thing to remember is that community depends on the individual, not on others, not on interaction, not on circumstances. It is what happens within the individual that creates community."

"That seems like a rather novel view of community, Kevin. I'm not sure what you mean."

"If someone lives in community with others, whether it be a family, a religious community, or any kind of human grouping in which there is interdependence, the person can never make his or her experience of bonding depend on externals. It depends on the attitude within the individual. How the externals of community are formed is determined by the attitude of the individual."

"Are you thinking of the interaction of the attitudes of each person in the group, Kevin?"

"Yes and no. In the end that will, of course, have an impact on the situation, but that is not what I am saying now. Community is within the person first. It can only exist as a dynamic interaction among persons if it is alive within the person ... even if it is alive within only one person in the group. That is the basic first element. No member of a community can say "I cannot find community here with this group of people," without admitting that he or she does not have community within. If true community exists within the person, it will exist in the bonding that person experiences with all created things: fire, water, trees, birds, and of course, persons. That is one of the messages of Francis of Assisi. He experienced the unity, community, of all nature and all persons because he had found community within himself."

"I'm beginning to understand what you mean, Kevin. The community within is a communion with one's true Self and a deepening union with the community of the Trinity dwelling within the person. Is that what you are saying?"

"That's right. To know yourself is to accept yourself and to be able to speak with and to listen to your deepest center, the image of God within you. It is to enter into the life and love of the Trinity. The consequence of meeting God within yourself is that your eyes are opened. You begin to see God in all that surrounds you. The bonding among persons in true community is actually an extension of the bonding of love within the Trinity. To form community or to develop any relationship is to break down barriers, to free the God within yourself to love himself in others. It is to liberate the dynamic energies of the Trinity within yourself to overflow into others' lives, to touch them with God's own love. Once that action begins, the response of others, in a sense, matters little. Your love, which is God's love, is no longer dependent upon a return of love. Yet, paradoxically, it is that very, unselfish disinterestedness on the part of the person which awakens the other and helps him or her to find community within, that community with the true self and with God which, in turn, overflows into others' lives."

"Then when you say that community depends on the attitude within the individual, you mean that that attitude acts as a catalyst which empowers others to be themselves."

"Yes, and it is only when each person in any relationship is able to be herself or himself that the person can stand free and open. The person then no longer has to put up barriers because he or she feels threatened by others. It is those protective barriers which prevent true relationships."

The most significant idea that came through to me in this dialogue was the key role that self-acceptance and individual maturity play in any relationship. Of course, it is true that one person can turn away and break a relationship, regardless of the wholeness and maturity of the other. A husband or wife may file for divorce, an old friend may suddenly stop speaking to me and refuse to discuss the reason. We are not always able to preserve or to reopen a relationship. Then too, we ourselves may choose not to continue it. But there are many relationships which are lasting and yet never seem to grow stronger. Instead, we can become so accustomed to them that we take them for granted and they survive in spite of frequent conflict or simple distancing. Members of a religious community or a husband and wife can simply co-exist and little by little find that they are leading separate lives even though they live under the same roof.

These are the situations in which it helps to examine what each individual brings to the marriage, friendship, family or community. If a person is divided within herself or himself, the person is insecure and, therefore, constructs protective barriers. The destruction of these barriers or, in psychological terms, of inappropriate personae is key to the formation of all relationships whether they be our relationship with God, with ourselves, or with others.

A point of clarification is necessary here. According to the psychological framework of Carl Jung, everyone fashions masks or personae to wear when playing different roles in life. An individual may develop a persona or behavior appropriate to a nurse, a father, a carpenter, a minister, a receptionist, and so forth. This is natural and helpful for social interaction. Too often, however, a person gradually identifies so strongly with the role he or she is playing that the individual forgets to take off the mask when it is not appropriate. It then becomes an artificial facade behind which the person hides, sometimes without realizing it. Then the persona becomes a barrier, and must be removed if there is to be true community with others.

We are sometimes afraid to let others see us as we really are because we are not sure they will like what they see. Our insecurity leads us at times to hide behind the protective barrier of our persona, for example, our profession, abilities, achievements, or status. We spend a lot of time and energy creating the personality we think will impress others. The result is a facade which conceals our true Self not only from others, but from ourselves. We come to believe the persona we have molded is who we really are. Then we proceed to bury our faults behind that facade. This works for a time, but eventually our foibles emerge when we least expect.

These are our shadows, another psychological term to describe our qualities, positive or negative, that lie so well hidden in the shadows or recesses of our unconscious that we are not aware of them. Psychologists point out that when these qualities of our personalities are repressed and not accepted as part of ourselves, they are projected onto other people. Our own pride may cause us to see someone else as opinionated and conceited. Our desire to be more at ease in a social situation may cause us to exaggerate and idolize that quality in another person. When I was in grade school, a teacher impressed upon me that what bothers us most in others is often our own greatest weakness. I did not understand that at the time, but it intrigued me enough that I still remember it. I would look at what irritated me in someone else and think, "I don't act that way." The truth is that I probably did, but I did not yet know myself well enough to discover my own weakness. If a friend was domineering or bossy, it would bother me and I would be glad I was not like her. Unfortunately, I was. I now realize that observing which faults or positive qualities I notice in others is a helpful tool in knowing myself better.

When we do not know ourselves well enough to identify, accept and integrate our shortcomings, we project them onto the very people with whom we are relating. We blame the other person rather than ourselves and our own projections for misunderstandings and irritations. If the other person would reform, things would go more smoothly. We will continue to see others as the culprits in causing unpleasant situations, conflicts and personal hurts until we can realize that often we are projecting our own feelings onto them, imagining that they are thinking what, in fact, we are thinking.

It is easy to console ourselves by reflecting that others, too, put up barriers and hide their real Self from us, so they

124

are at least partly to blame for a difficult or shallow relationship. They project their faults onto us just as much as we project ours onto them. While that may be true, to engage in that kind of rationalization is futile. It becomes an endless game of justifying our behavior by saying the other person is just as bad as we are.

The continual process of projection can only be broken by standing back and accepting full responsibility for a relationship with another. We must be able to admit, "It is my attitude which affects this relationship, this community." That does not only refer to my attitude toward the other persons, but first and foremost to my attitude toward myself. If I know myself, I am comfortable with myself; if I love myself with all of my faults as well as my virtues, it is safe to let down the barriers, take off my mask and relax. I may be more vulnerable, but I am no longer threatened by others. The amazing thing is that others gradually begin to feel more at ease and less threatened by me, so they also tentatively begin to come out from behind their facade and let me see them as they really are. Then a true relationship can begin. Up to this point it was a relationship between two people or among a group of people who did not really know themselves or each other, an artificial relationship at the level of the false persona, not at the level of the Self. It is important to remember, however, that I can never improve my attitude toward myself without also giving attention to my attitude toward God.

To return to the example of St. Paul, before his conversion he was so immersed in his role of Pharisee, one who upholds and preserves the law and tradition, that he forgot his real identity. His behavior fit the mold of his persona and he did what others expected of a good Pharisee. When he was blinded his persona was suddenly shattered. He found himself dependent upon others and, what was even more difficult, Jesus directed him to go into the Christian community and trust the very people whom he had been persecuting. Paul had no other recourse but to be himself. He had no place to hide. Only then was he able to stop projecting his own pride and self-righteousness onto the Christians. At first they were afraid of him, because they knew only his persona, but as they came to see him as he really was, they were no longer threatened by him and began to trust him. The relationship between Paul and the Christians was transformed because Paul's attitude changed. This happened because of a tremendous grace which enabled him to grasp the depth of the truth he had heard: "I am Jesus, and you are persecuting me." (Acts 9:6) Paul opened himself to the experience of the Word of God even though it meant risking a radical transformation, and thus he gradually assimilated the meaning and implications of Jesus' words: ". . . I am in my Father and you in me and I in you." (Jn 14:20)

As Paul came to know himself and accept himself, he was able to be honest with those whom he met, fellow Jews, Christians, and Gentiles. Honesty is another essential element in the deepening of any relationship. We are threatened by anyone whom we do not trust because we sense a lack of honesty, and, therefore, immediately put up our barriers. I was recently asked to give a talk to a group of single adults at a local church. Before I began, the leader suggested that as an ice-breaker each one give his or her name and mention the most important ingredient of a relationship. The quality mentioned most frequently was honesty. Many of them had probably had unfortunate experiences in which someone was not honest with them. We can only be honest if we have the courage to be ourselves. And how can we be ourselves if we do not even know our own shadows, and are unaware of our persona? Honesty begins with self-knowledge and implies a readiness to accept our good qualities as well as our faults.

As Christians we are called to be perfect as our heavenly Father is perfect, an awesome challenge! Created in the image of the Trinity, we can truly be ourselves only by patterning our lives on the community of the Trinity. This means that we are called to live our lives in a continual outpouring and receiving of love. In doing this we actually participate in the life of God. This is manifested in three dimensions: our love of God, ourselves, and others. We become, in fact, channels for the dynamic, constant love of the Trinity. Paul reminds us of this tremendous reality, "The charity of God is poured forth in our hearts by the Holy Spirit who has been given to us." (Rom 5:5)

At this point in our reflection we again enter the level of mystery. How can this be? Faith alone can answer that question. Jesus, by a total sharing in our humanity, raised us to share in his divinity. A realization of that truth can only come slowly, as we are prepared to accept its consequences which will move through our life, our choices, and our relationships just as the ripples on a pond created by one small pebble move outward in ever widening circles. At first we are tempted to turn away from the implications of really sharing in the life of God because of the responsibility which that entails. But then we remember that we are not alone. The night before his death Jesus reassured us, "I will not leave you orphans; I will come back to you." (Jn 14:18) He will accomplish this work in us.

The next time I notice a patch of shamrocks along the road or see a rack of St. Patrick's Day cards in the store I will again marvel at the simplicity of God's ways of revealing himself to us. We search for understanding in complex meditations and tomes of theology, and he is speaking to us all the while through the ordinary. The Spirit of truth is within us and Jesus told us, "The Holy Spirit whom the Father will send in my name will teach you everything and remind you of everything I have said to you." (Jn 14:26)

Epilogue

This afternoon, warmed by the winter sun, I sat high on a hill overlooking the immense pond we call ocean. Its silent, slate-blue surface seemed motionless except for a silver path etched by the waves dancing with the sunlight. I tossed imaginary pebbles into its depth wondering what movements they might create and where they would come to rest.

As I finish this book and toss its handful of pebbles into many different ponds, I wonder too what thoughts they might stir in the hearts of those who read of dandelions and shamrocks, merry-go-rounds and leprechauns.

I am reminded of the time a gas station attendant was washing the windshield of my car when he stopped and said to me, "You know, every time I see a can of sardines on the shelf I think of you." I was speechless. How does one respond to such a statement? "You do?" I questioned hesitantly. "Yes," he said, "I remember the talk you gave on Shrove Tuesday about Goya's painting, The Burial of the Sardine, and I think of what you said." I was immensely relieved to know why sardines made him think of me, and gratified to realize that the symbol still had the power to remind him of our need to empty ourselves and let go of extras in our lives that we might be filled with the joys of the resurrection.

I hope the symbols in this book will continue to speak to you also long after the paragraphs in between have been forgotten. Symbols resonate a personal message that can touch the heart in a unique way. Perhaps they will awaken the symbols of your own inner truth.

While writing these pages I have made friends with Moses, Elijah, Jonah and Daniel, Moses' mother, Eve and Adam. They are no longer simply people who lived in the far distant past, but they are with me in the parenthesis of the present moment. Perhaps they have also come alive to those who have read of their experiences, for these too are symbols with the capacity to join the truths of the past with present realities. Introduce yourself to others, Noah, Job, Esther, Paul, Anna and John. There are so many waiting to speak to you. Let them toss some pebbles into your still pond, and then quietly watch the ripples continue to skim across the surface as the pebble sinks into a special niche in your heart. You will find that your reserve of pebbles is endless.